The CLICK Technique

Tap into the Internet's Massive Power to Produce a Steady Stream of Traffic and Leads for Your Small Business

By Lindsey Anderson,
"One-Click Lindsey"
Digital Marketing Expert

The CLICK Technique
Tap into the Internet's Massive Power to Produce a Steady Stream of Traffic and Leads for Your Small Business

Published by OCL Publishing
2850 SW Cedar Hills Blvd.
#120
Beaverton, OR 97005

ISBN: 978-1-7323976-0-6

Cover design by Jim Saurbaugh

reader of this publication assumes responsibility for the use of these materials and information. Adherence to all applicable laws and regulations, both advertising and all other aspects of doing business in the United States or any other jurisdiction, is the sole responsibility of the purchaser or reader.

This book is intended to provide accurate information with regards to the subject matter covered. However, the Author and the Publisher accept no responsibility for inaccuracies or omissions, and the Author and Publisher specifically disclaim any liability, loss, or risk, whether personal, financial, or otherwise, that is incurred as a consequence, directly or indirectly, from the use and/or application of any of the contents of this book.

Table of Contents

Foreword

You might think you're holding a book about online marketing, but you'd be wrong. This book is more of a roadmap on how you can to use the massive power of the internet to attract a steady stream of customers and prospects.

Seems like a big promise, so let me explain.

In a world filled with far too many self-proclaimed experts and gurus, Lindsey Anderson is the real deal. She's known internationally as "One-Click" Lindsey (you'll learn why in the book), and together with her all-star team, she is the hidden gem behind some of today's biggest websites and online campaigns.

Lindsey's classic trademarked phrase, *"The answer to your slow growth is just one click away"* really says it all. As more and more businesses rely on the internet and their websites to do some of the heavy lifting of new customer acquisition, websites that fail to get visitors to make at least a single click are failing.

As an author and small business coach, I frequently am asked to review and recommend books. As much as it is an honor to be asked, I have to say no to most requests purely based on my busy schedule. When my friend and client, Lindsey Anderson, asked if I would review her book, *The CLICK Technique*, based on how much I admire and respect Lindsey for what she's accomplished in her career and how much she has personally helped my company grow with her knowledge of online marketing, I immediately said yes!

Allow me to share just one of the profit nuggets you'll learn in *The CLICK Technique* that I know you will find ultra-valuable. The letter "C" stands for curiosity. Lindsey astutely points out that nearly all of the traffic to your website happens because someone, a potential customer perhaps, is "curious" about something. Ninety-nine percent of the visitors to your web site are *not* looking to buy something. Instead, they're curious about finding an answer to whatever problem your company might be able to solve. Understanding and solving this piece of the puzzle is the starting point to a great website, and getting this wrong means almost certain disaster as it relates to ROI.

A dose of reality: There is a statistic that's been around for decades that indicates 80 percent of small businesses fail within the first five years. Of those that survive – far too many only "exist" and, despite hard work, never prosper. One of the reasons for this, I believe, is that far too many small business owners try to do everything themselves, and, in an effort to save a buck, they waste far more time and money being completely ineffective. I know this to be true because I did the same thing many years ago when I was starting my online businesses.

Lindsey and her team at TrafficandLeads.com have built several of my company's websites and today, they run all of my online marketing campaigns. The good news is if you want to learn how the internet can truly work for entrepreneurs, and even try some strategies on your own, *The CLICK Technique* is the best book I've ever read that explains the process.

I highly suggest reading and learning these important foundational principles in *The CLICK Technique*, even if you end up hiring Lindsey to help your company grow!

Jim Palmer - The Dream Business Coach
www.GetJimPalmer.com

Foreword

Why You Need This Book

Consider the entrepreneur who launched their business relying on digital marketing because they were told and believed there was an endless supply of leads – potential customers who would buy their product or service, making their business wildly successful. With an endless supply of leads, making their entrepreneurial and financial dreams come true would be a slam dunk. This endless supply of leads was (and is) referred to as "traffic." They saw it first hand on the internet; they heard the success stories. They thought it would be easy. Perhaps you are that entrepreneur.

The internet leveled the playing field for small businesses, right? Yes! Even the smallest entrepreneur can play like one of the big boys, thanks to online marketing, right? Yes! Everyone's online these days, either shopping or at least researching their purchases, right? Yes! Anyone can do it, right? Yes!

So you've studied everything you could find about online marketing and spent plenty of money building a killer website... and the result is... well, the result is not at all what you expected. Perhaps your story is a lot like Darren's:

Darren runs a highly successful weight loss clinic. The success of the clinic can be attributed to a piece of software he spent years creating that will produce individualized eating plans to help clients lose weight. If you've ever tried to lose weight, you know it's no easy task. Even if you've never tackled weight loss, you've no doubt seen countless ads from countless programs all practically guaranteeing easy success. The weight loss sector is highly competitive, and there is quite a lot of traffic in that realm. It seems practically everyone is seeking help with weight loss at one time or another.

Despite the failure of many weight loss programs and clinics, Darren's approach was different and really did produce results for his clients. In fact, Darren's clinic was so successful, he decided to take it to the masses and allow everyone who was struggling with their weight to take advantage of these amazing eating plans. Why not? The amount of traffic (i.e., leads and potential customers) searching for weight loss programs on the internet was truly astronomical. So, he dove in, posted on Facebook, wrote some articles, and waited for people to sign up for his product. Guess what? No one did. There was all of this traffic, but none of it steered in Darren's direction.

Darren finally contacted me... and we went to work. We set up Facebook Ads, did search engine optimization (SEO) to capitalize on the keywords potential customers were using, created a content strategy and an irresistible offer for a copy of his weight loss book, and created an online marketing lead generation machine. Then Darren got the results he was looking for, and a lot of his clients are leaner and lighter as a result.

Traffic is only the first step. Consider the brick-and-mortar store on a busy road. Plenty of traffic passes by every day, and potential customers may see the signs and think the store looks nice, but if no one stops in... well, you quickly get the picture: no sales. The internet works exactly the same way. Sure, there's plenty of traffic, but to be successful, you need to cut through the clutter and drive the traffic *you want* to your site and ultimately to your small business. The notion of "a lot of traffic" in and of itself is no more helpful to you than the line of cars passing by that brick-and-mortar business. Always driving by, never stopping. It certainly isn't doing anything for your bottom line.

If this is your dilemma, first don't feel bad. You aren't alone. I've seen – and helped – countless entrepreneurs who bought into the idea that the internet created a level playing field and if they simply put up a website – a professional-looking website – the world would beat a path to their door. Almost each one of them wasted a ton of money... and a ton of time – time they could have spent really growing their businesses. It wasn't their fault, and if you're in the same boat, it's not your fault either.

Successful digital marketing can be difficult on the easiest of days, and, to make it even more complex, it's changing, and it's changing All. The. Time.

You need people to find you... and find you quickly online. (A big consequence of internet speed: We now expect *everything* in seconds!) Once they land on your site, they have to immediately understand what you can do for them and be able to click to get the result they want and the sale you want. That's exactly why I've created The CLICK Technique. If... if... if you know how to do it, everything you've heard about successful digital marketing is absolutely true, and your small business can compete with anyone and everyone. If you know how to do it, the incredible growth of your business *can* be just one click away!

Why One-Click Lindsey?

I started my general web development business in Idaho Falls, Idaho in 2005. At the time, I was working at a Department of Energy site out in the middle of the desert as a contractor testing the software that tracked drums full of nuclear waste. We made a lot of money working out there, but the work was really boring. So I decided to start a side hustle and Web Impakt, my web development company was born. (Yes... with a K. I would have much rather named that company "Web Impact," but webimpact.com was not available. As a result, I've spent the last 10 years telling people "Web Impakt...

with a 'K'.") Okay, so back to the point. The point is the web development business was (and still is) tough. Everyone knows at least five people who develop websites, so we were constantly competing on price, which – as you likely know – doesn't make it easy to make a profit.

"I need customers!"

If you are reading this, then you are either my mother or you have the same thought always sitting in the back of your head: "I need customers!" Over a decade ago, when I decided to start my web development company, these three words consumed me. I had a few good clients that I acquired while I was in the "moonlighting" phase of my business, but renting an office, buying equipment, and hiring employees brought this pressure to a whole new level. So, what was my strategy to bring in a sustainable stream of new prospects and customers that would give my business the nutrition it needed to grow?

A great website showing off my company's work was my first step. Surely that would convince people to bring their website needs to me, right? I hired a salesperson immediately. After all, a professional salesperson must have the skills to make cold calling and dropping in on businesses a successful venture. Leads purchased online, radio advertisements, having my business sponsor community events around town... surely all of this would get business coming in, right? Well, the first several years of running my business included learning some very difficult lessons. A website is only as good as the traffic that goes to it. My salespeople, more often than not, had no better ideas than I did about where to go for prospects. (In fact, they continually turned to me for leads!) Purchased leads were either bogus or pounced on by dozens of other companies. Nothing I tried seemed like it was a dependable way to bring in new work.

I finally realized that folks don't just want a website. Sure, at the start of the Digital Age, it was the thing to have. Being able to spout off your URL was like a badge of honor. However, websites were and still are utterly unless they are generating clients or, as I like to say, "traffic and leads." Lo and behold, I took to GoDaddy and picked up that domain name and my online marketing company was born. We still do a lot of web development and custom programming on the Web Impakt side of the house, but my real passion lies with digital marketing. I can make traffic and leads flow into any and every business I can get my hands on.

Flash forward: There is a chiropractor in the office next door, and he's ready to generate some traffic and leads. The doc is a really nice guy but a tad impatient. As I've always said, traffic and leads take a bit of time to generate. I happen to walk into the office at the same time he does. Every. Single. Morning. The conversation would be the same: "Hey Doc!"

"Hey... so I haven't seen any leads come in yet."

This happened day after day, and my response would be, "Yep! Working on all the steps that I need to do to get prospects to make that '**One Click**'... and once they do that and join your email list, they will be your patient the moment they are serious about looking for a chiro in the area."

Finally, one evening, I slipped into the office while walking past and made a change to the landing page and went home to bed. The next morning, lo and behold if we didn't have 20 new emails on his list! That morning, while drinking my Starbucks, we met at the front door as usual and he said, "Well, well, well... if it isn't 'One-Click Lindsey'."

I liked the sound of that, so I adopted it and have been called "One-Click Lindsey," "OCL," or "One-Click" ever since. It works. I frequently speak at conferences or on podcasts and am always referred to and remembered as this. It's a little marketing trick, and it works like a charm.

We work hard on traffic and leads, and I created a process that we now put all of our clients through. Some of our clients pay us to implement small parts of the technique while others pay us monthly to execute the entire thing for them. I sat down and formulated this secret and highly effective tactic that will produce an endless stream of traffic and leads for my clients for years to come. It's exactly what I am going to share with you in this book.

WARNING: Please be warned that I am not going to tell you about a get-rich-quick scheme that will land you six-figure launches in a week or make you a millionaire next year. What I am promising you is that if you follow this technique and you stick with it, six months from now, you'll thank me. You'll be off that constant up and down roller coaster of having enough leads and then not having any... because you're servicing the leads that you have! The CLICK Technique is the *cornerstone* of all online marketing. You can do so many other things once you have this foundation in place. But like building a solid house, you have to start with the right foundation. Yes, building a foundation takes time, but it is the most critical aspect of building a house... or a business... that will stand the test of time.

The CLICK Technique combines piquing your prospects' curiosity, having a great landing page and irresistible offer, then cultivating the relationship... and you gotta' keep going. Once you have such a foundation, the six-figure launches will be possible. You can have never-ending traffic and leads, and you can finally stop wondering where your next client is coming from. Without having to continually chase clients, you will have the luxury of time to truly expand your business and boost your bottom line.

If you're ready to do just that, let's get started!

Why You Need This Book

Chapter 1

Curiosity

Think of all of the content that you are now exposed to every day. Every. Single. Day. There is no escaping it. From the moment I wake up, I grab my phone, glance at the dozens of emails that have come in overnight. I turn on cable news, where I not only get to watch the breaking story of the moment but can instantly check the bottom ticker for the weather, time, stock market, and dozens of other stories rotating by. Facebook, Twitter, Instagram feeds, YouTube subscriptions... it just goes on and on and on and.... As the amount of content to which people are exposed grows, the available time that a person has to actually focus on a single piece of content becomes an increasingly precious resource. You know that to be true because you are inundated with content all day, every day. How do I know that? Because you are a human being on this planet with access to media.

The problem for many small businesses is that they do not take this attention economy into account when they venture into social media to promote their business. After all, as I'm scrolling through my Facebook feed and see a post announcing that John's Widgets are 10 percent off right above an adorable video of my friend's cat sneezing, then John and his widgets are never given a second thought.

Does that mean that all hope is lost when it comes to capturing the attention of your prospective clients? Not at all. It simply means that the spoils are going to go to the marketer who understands this attention economy and its impact on prospects. But before we go any further, let's start at the beginning....

Content: Required, Not Optional

The CLICK Technique is based on a very important psychological principle: People will do business with people who they feel they know and like... and trust. Several times a day, I have somebody sign up for a consultation with me to find out how to make their online marketing work better. After I do an examination of their online presence, it's very rare that I don't tell the person that they need to create a lot more content for their blog, social media, and email campaigns. It's probably not a big surprise that a lot of these people grimace at this suggestion. I can hear their frustration as they protest that they have nothing to say, or no time to say it, or that they don't think it would work for them. I can tell that many of them were desperately hoping that I had the secret sauce to bypass this somewhat irritating aspect of online marketing. But I don't, and nobody else does, either.

It's the content that you create that gives social media marketing its power; there is simply no way around it. Without content, you might as well just do some "plain vanilla" search engine optimization or pay-per-click advertising and hope for the best. (And hope really, really hard because this can get really expensive if not executed correctly.)

It's the content you create that tells the story of your services or your products, that introduces you to these potential customers, and that makes the people you are reaching feel comfortable opening their wallets and giving you their business.

That isn't to say I don't understand my client's hesitation. Content creation can be a soul-crushing experience! It can be so frustrating to write a blog post to which no one responds or comments, to send out newsletters and only see notices of people clicking "unsubscribe," or

> *Content drives the success of The CLICK Technique as well as the overall success of your online marketing and business!*

to post a video that people watch for 15 seconds... or less. Not only that and when you're just getting your feet wet, the creation of the content can take *so* much time! I used to spend a day going back and forth on a blog, or spend more than a day writing a script and shooting and editing a video. To put that kind of time into something that you feel didn't produce results can sour anybody on content creation.

The people who are successful are the people who can push through this. The people who show up on *Shark Tank* who say they posted something on Facebook and their business exploded are the exceptions to the rule that, most of the time, social media marketing success means grinding it out and slowly building up your audience. One of the main qualities that turns an athlete into an Olympian is the ability to maintain the day in and day out monotony of training. This important internal motivation and self-direction is what sets Olympians apart from regular athletes. This same trait – the ability to stick with it day in and day out – is also what sets successful digital marketers apart from the thousands of entrepreneurs who start their journey into digital marketing but stop because they don't succeed immediately. (And these entrepreneurs are also typically the ones whose businesses fail.)

What Do You Say?

Once I get people over the hurdle of understanding that they *have to* create content, I have to get them to understand that it's more than that. They have to create *interesting* content. After struggling with my clients or members of my private Facebook group (clicktechniquegroup.com) to create content, I usually have to train them to actually write interesting content. I can't tell you how many times somebody has told me, "There is nothing interesting about my business."

To that, I want to ask, "Then why are you in it? Why do you spend every day in your business if it's not interesting?" I'm certain it's not **uninteresting**, but there has to be a mindset shift. Any business that is worthy of being around has something interesting that can be said about it. You just have to view it from the perspective of your customer. In other words, you have to get out of your own head and into your prospect's head to figure out what they'll find interesting. You have to understand their pain point and how you are solving their problem. Once I can get them viewing their business from that perspective, they actually enjoy creating their content more!

A perfect example is one of my clients – Matt, who is your "average, ordinary" insurance agent. Matt was excited about using social media to get more clients but was pretty insistent that there was absolutely no way that what he did could be made into interesting content. I asked Matt why people chose him for insurance rather than other insurance agents in the area. "Well, usually people just shop based on price. Either that or people I know from around town or friends of friends seek me out to help them."

I was confident that The CLICK Technique would work perfectly for him; he just had to give people the chance to get to know him by telling them something interesting! I worked with Matt on an idea about which he was definitely skeptical. I suggested a series of short videos explaining aspects of an auto insurance policy and what questions to ask your insurance agent. These videos were quick, to the point, and allowed Matt to smile into the camera and allow people to get to know him. The videos didn't suggest, "Come to me! I'll sell you this great insurance!" They were more along the lines of: "Here's some good information you should know. Be sure to ask your agent if you're covered!" Not only that but Matt was dedicated to blogging and emailing his list. The content all had the same feel to it: "Things an insurance agent knows that you need to know, too."

This worked great for Matt. There were times when he would actually call me and say, "We need to stop; I have too many new prospects coming in. I'm overwhelmed!" It's always a great feeling when I have to give my client a pep talk that they can handle all of the new work! We found a pace that kept his audience

There are countless ways to develop topics for your content that your prospects will find interesting and that will drive their curiosity to learn more.

engaged and brought in just a bit more than he thought he could handle. And in case you've forgotten the point: He did this by finding what made *insurance* interesting and in a way that piqued the curiosity of his prospects to want to learn more!

So, what content can you create that will make your potential clients curious enough to spend a minute or so of their day with you? Giving away your industry's secrets is a great place to start! I do it myself... right here in this book and all over the place online. Are you a plumber? Post a video showing somebody how to fix a jammed garbage disposal with a broom handle. A life coach? Tell people to go through their inbox, create a to-do list, and file them away. A carpet cleaner? Show people how to get a red wine stain out themselves. Sure, you might lose the opportunity to do that small job, but your audience will trust you and view you as the expert in the field.

Years ago, I wrote a blog post about whether Wix (an online build-it-yourself website tool – obviously a competitor to my own business at the time) was a good option for a small business. A lot of businesses just starting out don't have thousands of dollars to spend on a website, so could a free tool really be good enough? My conclusion: Yup; Wix gets an A in my book for being able to provide a decent website for a small business with a tight budget. Right after posting it, wammo bammo, I was flooded with messages and calls asking me, "Uh, aren't you doing websites anymore? I saw you telling people to just use Wix." The fact was I wasn't interested in selling my services to a young business that may be better off with Wix simply to pad my bottom line! Use Wix, grow your business, and then when you're outgrowing that platform, remember who was looking out for you and helped you get off the ground!

One more thing about content: It not only has to be interesting, it has to be *consistent*. My guess is that you are thinking, "I probably have enough ideas for a couple months, what then?" This was the problem facing my chiropractor client. He'd done some content on posture, lifting heavy things, beneficial stretches you could do. He had pretty much plucked all of the low-hanging fruit that he could reach and was convinced there was nothing else he could tell people. We ventured out to Quora, which is a question-and-answer site where people ask questions that are answered by a community of users. After a quick search, he discovered that there were a lot of chiropractic-related questions that he didn't even know people were asking! Things like:

- "Is it worth going to a chiropractor if there is no pain?"
- "Do children need chiropractors?"
- "How long does it take to get results from a chiropractor?"
- "Can my pet benefit from a chiropractor?"

The list went on and on. It was chock full of ideas for him to consistently create content. Reddit is another great site on which people will post questions about countless topics.

Remember this: There is a lot you can say about your business, way more than you might imagine because you are usually too close to your business and cannot see it from the perspective of your prospects. The more you work at putting yourself out there, the easier all of this content creation will be. Put your head down and do it!

Oh... But Use Keywords or It'll Be Useless

There is one other aspect to keep in mind when you're creating your content: keywords. I know, I know. I steered you right into the world of Google and search engine optimization; sorry, but it's important. The best traffic you are going to get to discover your content will be organic traffic from Google (and the other search engines, but... come on... Google). Organic traffic means people who have come to your content by searching for something on Google and following one of those search results to your content as opposed to people who already knew about your company and searched for you directly. These folks are the perfect people to snag for your list because they are actively searching for what you are saying... and selling.

Consider this example of effectively uncovering and then leveraging key words: Mary came to me completely frazzled with her efforts in online marketing. I don't blame her. This amazing gal was blogging three times a week and had been for nearly eight years! Here's the math on that: 1,248 blogs. When I popped in and looked at her analytics, the results were dire. She had about 50 people a week coming to her site. You've heard content is king, and Mary was putting out content like a queen, but it *was not working*. What was the problem?

Mary sold products in the Christianity niche. She was a life coach and sold products to improve the lives of women who were dedicated to raising their families with religious virtues. Her blog posts centered on family and faith. The problem was that she wasn't using any words that people were actually searching for on Google. Let me give you an example: She wrote a blog post entitled, "It's More than Just Sweatpants." This engaging blog post detailed how manners and civility are more than just dressing appropriately. The title may pique your curiosity; however, when folks are on Google searching for "teaching children manners," they aren't typing in "sweatpants and civility." So we popped in and made some on-page adjustments to the wording to match what people were actually searching for on Google. After a few weeks of Google indexing the site and doing its thing, she started showing up!

Quick note: SEO is much more complex than this, but in this instance, doing some on-page changes was just enough to get Google and the other search engines to notice her.

What is it exactly that your customer is looking for? And what words are they using to search? Are you sure? Don't be too quick to make an assumption based on your own perspective. Remember that prospects probably see your business a bit differently. Doing a little bit of research into the keywords that your intended audience is using when searching for your product or service is crucial, not only for carrying out a search engine optimization

> *If you fail to view your business from your prospects' and customers' perspectives, you are hobbling your ability to grow and be profitable.*

campaign but also for content creation. You might think you know what people are searching for, but you'd be surprised how often a few choice words can make the difference between content that people are flocking to versus the stuff they are ignoring.

Let's say, for example, that my chiropractic client wanted to target people searching for "chiropractic services." That seems reasonable enough (and he should target that keyword), but after doing a smidge of keyword research, you will find that people are searching for "chiropractic services," but they are also searching "holistic medicine," "subluxation," and "are chiropractors safe." These sound like perfect blog post topics, ***and*** if you utilize these keywords appropriately, you can actually start ranking for them. It may not seem like a big deal, but a small change like that will let Google know what your content is about, and they will reward you by increasing your search engine rankings.

The good news is that – no matter the size of your business – you have one of the biggest companies in the world on your side. Google has actually created a tool that will help you find the perfect keywords to use. Pretty nice that a multi-billion-dollar company is just sitting around waiting for their chance to help you out, isn't it? Go to Google and google "Google Keyword Planner." (I just wanted to see how many times I could use Google in a sentence!) Type in the keywords you *think* folks are going to be using. Google will let you know how many people per month are looking for that particular word or phrase and will suggest some other words or phrases that are similar and let you know how many people are searching for those! Google Insights (again... just google it) will tell you even more about these keywords, including how they have been trending in the search engine for the past few years.

An SEO Primer

You've probably heard the term SEO or search engine optimization, but I want to share a quick lesson on Google. While I've been using "Google" and as I use it throughout the remainder of the book, I'm referring all search engines like Bing and Yahoo!, not just that one.

As a search engine, Google's entire purpose is to make sure that they show the ***most relevant*** results to the searcher. If you to go Google and suddenly the results show you a bunch of dog brushes when you typed in "cat dish," then you wouldn't go to Google to perform your searches any more, now would you? Therefore, it's paramount that your blog is full of creative and useful content that solves the problems and questions for which people are searching. If you are offering up the answers to these questions, then Google is going to naturally allow you to rise in the search engine rankings.

According to Matt Cutts, a leading software developer at Google, Google uses "over" 200 factors in determining who ranks first in the search engines and that each of these factors has numerous variations. That sounds complicated, and to make matters worse, Google doesn't publish the factors. It's up to search engine optimization companies like mine to test and study in order to try to figure out the best factors that drive the results. I could make this entire book about SEO, but I won't. Instead, I am

> *Google is well aware of all of the "tricks" people use to try to improve their rank on search results pages. Quality content and relevant links will always work.*

going to narrow it down to a few factors you need to know.

On-page vs. Off-page SEO: There are two types of SEO. On-page SEO comprises the things you do on your website, including the use of keywords in your content and metadata that ensure that search engines know what your page is about. Off-page SEO is made up of the things you do outside of your website, like link building and social media posting, that alerts search engines about your existence and how popular your content is.

Keyword Rich Content: When you develop content for your site, there are a few places where you need to place your keyword, including:

1. The Title Tag: The title tag can be found on each page of your website. If you visit a page on your website and look at the top of the browser, you will be able to see what your title tag is. You will find it between the <title> </title> in the code. Put your keywords here.

2. H1 Tag: While you are writing your blog posts, you want to make sure your section headings are located between the following tags <H1></H1>.

3. Page Copy: It's paramount that you use your keyword and variants of your keyword throughout your page copy.

Backlinks: A backlink is an incoming hyperlink from another website. For example: If you were a podcast guest and the podcast host included a link to your website in the show notes, that would be considered a backlink. Backlinks are a very integral part of the SEO puzzle. In general, for every site that has a link pointing back to your site, Google considers that as a vote of confidence that your website is legit with great information. Therefore, the more links that point back to you, the higher you will rank on the search engine results page. There are a few things to remember before you head out to Fiverr.com or someplace similar and get an overseas contractor to create a million backlinks for you for $5. Google also considers the source of the backlink and requires that it's a "quality" site with "good" information that is somehow related to what is on your site. Google bots are really smart (and Google works tirelessly to continue their education), so don't try to trick the system by buying backlinks or trying to get crappy backlinks from across the web.

For many years, Google has told all online marketers to *stop focusing on building links!* However, there is a ton of research by highly esteemed companies like MOZ.com that have proven that sites without backlinks won't rank, and it's safe to interpret Google's drum beat to stop building links to mean "earn links in a natural way."

All of this being said, you need to have links pointing back to your site. The best ways to do this include guest posting, reaching out to reference blogs and offering your link to be included, and writing and promoting amazing content that people will naturally link to as they are reading.

Easier said than done but those are the facts. It always comes back to making sure you have high quality content. High quality content will generate links.

I know that SEO can be really complex and is a constantly moving target. However, if you are using a WordPress website, which I highly recommend, again, there is a free plug-in called Yoast SEO. If you install this, all you need to do is enter a keyword and Yoast will walk you through everything you need to do to make sure that your blog post or page is ready for prime time.

Different Types of Content

So now that you know you need to create content and you have an idea on how to use that content to make people curious about you and you know how to tailor that content to reach the biggest group of people you can, what type of content can and should you create?

Blogging can be difficult to do and time-consuming, but it is *so* essential. Basically, a blog is a collection of articles (for lack of a better word) that you write and publish online. It can be difficult to consistently create entertaining and engaging blogs, but they'll attract organic traffic like nobody's business. Search engines just love digging into those meaty blog posts and scanning them for content.

Videos engage an audience like few other things can. I am constantly telling my clients to *do video*, and the resistance I get to that is difficult to overcome, but it's understandable. I get it. I was guilty. I *hated* doing videos when I started out. My husband and I would psych ourselves up for the long night of video shooting all week, and on Saturday, we'd put the kids to bed, I'd get all fancied up, and we'd head downstairs and start filming. I'd fumble through my prepared lines only to have my husband make the "Boy, that's the delivery you're going with?" face.

Then hours were spent editing all of the footage to put together something that I didn't cringe at when watching. Have I convinced you that videos are great yet? Well, it took some time, but it did get easier and easier. Eventually, I became less camera shy, I found my voice, and I felt comfortable letting my personality show through. Editing became easier and easier the more comfortable I became and the fewer fumbled lines I had to cut around. The simple fact is that people *need* to get to know you, and video is one of the best platforms to make that happen. Don't think your videos have to be huge productions either; just pull out your smartphone and a selfie stick and go to town. I don't care how you do it. Just get a video on your website and social media pages!

Live video is a new thing as I write this, and it can be more terrifying than simply posting a video that you can edit and over which you have greater control, but I've grown to love it. Social media sites like Facebook and Instagram allow you to broadcast live video and allow people to view, comment, and react to it in real time. It's such a great way to connect with your audience, and I mean really connect with them. Don't get hung up watching people join your video only to leave three seconds later. Even if nobody is around watching the video while you're broadcasting it, it'll still remain on your feed, and the practice of talking live on camera is never a bad thing.

Podcasting is my favorite type of content to produce. Podcasting, for those of you who are late to the party, is basically a radio show that you create and publish. Content delivery services such as iTunes will then deliver your new show to your subscribers. I have produced hundreds of episodes of my podcast "Traffic & Leads Podcast" during which I interview different people about different aspects of generating traffic and leads to your website and other aspects of online marketing. It's *so* easy for me to ask people questions, especially about something I'm interested in! Even better, I then take the recording and send it off to my team to have show notes made, which can then double as some of my written content for the week!

Depending on your business, photography might be the most crucial kind of content for you. Sites like Instagram are built for photographs, but whose eyes aren't drawn to a beautiful picture when it scrolls past you on your Twitter or Facebook feed? The main thing you have to remember about photography is that it has to look professional. If the lighting isn't right, or if the shot isn't framed well, or if it's a little blurry, then you really run the risk of looking like an amateur. If the crown jewel of my content was photography, I would spend some serious money on a camera and take a class to learn to use it properly, or else I'd hire a professional.

Warm and Cold Audiences

Regarding traffic: There are three types or shall I say temperatures of website traffic in this world – cold, warm, and hot, and it is important, especially when you're putting money behind your content, to tailor your traffic to the warmth of your audience.

Cold traffic is made up of people coming to your page who have never heard of you. They are doing research or clicked on an ad because you were lucky enough to pique their interest and curiosity. These casual browsers are difficult to sell to, so you have to warm them up by showing them blog posts, videos, podcasts, and other content items that will help them get to know your brand.

Warm traffic contains friendlier folks – podcast listeners, email subscribers, or peeps you've pixeled and are luring back to your website. While these folks may be warm and friendly, they still haven't purchased anything from you. Your goal with this audience is to get them to make a purchase or get them closer to that goal. Good places to send warm traffic include irresistible offers, demos, webinars, and trials.

Finally, hot traffic is made up of your current "happy" clients. In other words, they know you, they know your services, and chances are if you have a new offering that meets their needs, they will probably purchase again from you. You can take *hot* traffic and sell, sell, sell to them: Send them to sales pages, landing pages, service pages, or any place they can *buy* something!

That is driving curiosity through content in a nutshell, but let's circle back to where we started this chapter. Keep in mind that I didn't share all the stuff in this chapter to help you create content. *I did so to help you create content that will make people curious enough to spend some of their precious attention on that content and curious enough to get to know the creator of that content.*

Curious enough to maybe see what else that person has to offer. This content should really be viewed as your time to shine, to show off, to get people curious about wanting to know more about you because that is where it all starts. "Curiosity killed the cat," you say? To that, my response is, "But satisfaction brought it back!"

Once their curiosity has finally convinced them that the next logical step is to dig a little deeper into what it is that you have to offer, you'll need a place for them to go, so I guess we'd better cover that in the next chapter.

Get 'Em Clicking!

- We live in an attention economy and we all have limited time to give any attention to the content that inundates us every day.
- People will only do business with you if they know, like, and trust you. Content is your way to make that happen. It is not optional.
- If you want to be successful in your business, you need content. There is no other way.
- We're often too close to our own businesses to see what's interesting to prospects. Look for ways to expand your perspective to develop content that drives curiosity.

- Keywords: Don't shy away from them. There's a gold mine in them that reveals how prospects may be searching for your products and services.

- That billion-dollar business, Google, is actually willing to help every business of every size leverage the best keywords. Learn to use tools like Google Keyword Planner and Google Insights.

- Content can be shared in numerous ways like blogging, videos, and podcasts. The "right answer" regarding which to use is very likely a combination of all three.

Chapter 2

Landing

Now that you've piqued their curiosity and stoked their interest, you have to give them a nice, smooth place to land. You certainly don't want to bump them around the runway, now do you?

First, let me ask you: What is a landing page? If you answered that it's your main business website, you'd actually be incorrect. (But don't worry, that answer won't count toward your final grade because a lot of people get it wrong!)

Think of your main business website as your online marketing cornerstone. It's the main location where people go to find out more about your business when they are looking for information about you, your company, and the products and services you offer. It features the classic menu items like Home, About, Contact Us, Products etc. Your main website tends to be what populates on a Google search result page and where you direct potential and current clients for more information.

This "come on in, look around, have a fresh cookie while you peruse our offerings" is *not* the purpose of a landing page. A landing page is a very calculated, perfectly executed page with one… and *only one* goal. It's like the *Terminator* of selling on the web (hopefully without the '90s catch phrases).

A landing page covers a single topic and prompts the user to carry out a single call to action. People arrive at this landing page as the result of a very specific marketing medium, such as a pay-per-click campaign, search engine optimization, or Facebook or other social media posts or advertising.

Landing pages are all about specificity: One topic and one call to action.

The advertisements and keywords used in these campaigns are chosen to drive a very specific prospect with a very specific need to this very specific page. Have I mentioned? It's *specific!* You will typically have one main website for your business and could potentially have hundreds of landing pages. The landing pages aren't necessarily menu items on your website. In fact, website visitors will probably have no clue that most of them exist.

Let's look at an example: You're a business coach and you want to attract small business owners who are experiencing issues with marketing, team building, finance, and mindset. First, you would set up your main website that would feature your blogs, podcasts, videos, information about your programs, and testimonials. Secondarily, you may set up a landing page featuring a webinar you would be hosting entitled, "Improving Your Mindset." You would be driving folks to this webinar sign-up landing page through a PPC (pay-per-click) campaign, SEO, or Facebook Ads. The landing page for the webinar would feature only information about the webinar, and your only goal would be for someone to enter their name and email to get on the webinar list.

You would not take this opportunity to talk about all of the other great services you offer or anything else that does not directly address the prospect's current need – signing up for the mindset webinar. If they decide after hitting your landing page to Google your company and visit your company's website, that's great. And at that point, they can discover that you also help with finance and team building, and offer three types of small business coaching support programs.

The purpose of the landing page in this example is to stop, look your prospect in the eye, and say, "I know you have mindset issues, and I am the expert at small business mindset. Join me at my webinar for the answer to your mindset issues." So during the L phase of the "Land" part of The CLICK Technique, I want to address a few really important things that actually apply to both your main website and landing pages.

Must Haves for Anywhere Your Customer Lands

Regardless of whether your prospect is arriving at your landing page (on which they will only be presented with information about a single specific topic and can only take a single action) or on any page of your main business website, there are elements common to both of these landing opportunities that are critical for you to have. So before I jump into the real "nuts-and-bolts" specifics of a landing page, I want to address these first.

Professional Look and Feel

Your website must look professional and be well-designed. Unfortunately, regardless of what your mama said, people are going to judge a book... er... a website by its cover. You have mere milliseconds for people to make a judgement call about your website. If it's not professional looking, they will simply click away and find a competitor that will instill confidence (with *their* professional-looking and well-designed site) and provide to them what they are looking for. With the multitude of website builders available like Wix, Squarespace, and a plethora of WordPress templates, there is no reason to have an ugly website. End. Of. Story.

My company, Traffic and Leads, has built hundreds of websites. The main reason websites are blah instead of awesome is because of content. Some clients don't spend time on content, or they allow the site to go live with minimal or unprofessional content. We have copywriters on staff, and I often plead with clients to

There is no reason whatsoever in this day and age to have a shoddy looking website!

allow us to develop their "About Us" page or product pages, but when we're met with the attitude that content isn't important, I know the site will not be as great as it can be. Spend time on both the content and images on your site. This also applies to your landing pages. They must be professional for The CLICK Technique to work.

Google Analytics

Google Analytics is software provided by Google that will give you a massive amount of data about the traffic visiting your site. It will provide you with analytical information that you never thought to ask about or that you even needed. Examples include how many people visited your site, how they got there, where they clicked, and how long they stayed. While that information is critical, that is only the most basic type of data you will be able to glean from Google Analytics. You can also learn site visitors' geographic location, what files were downloaded, which pages are poorly performing, which keywords worked best, which online campaigns worked best, what visitors are searching for once they are on your site, your top content… and I am still only scratching the surface. The coolest part is that it's absolutely free! Simply go to Google and type "Google Analytics," and the directions will walk you through the rest. Essentially, all you have to do is snag the small piece of code they provide and place it in the header file of your website so that it appears on all the pages of your site. Your site visitors don't actually see this code, but it's working very hard behind the scenes.

Using Google Analytics is paramount for your success as an online marketer. Why? Because if we can't measure it, then we can't improve it. You have to know what's broken before you can fix it. Conversely, when you know what's working really, really well, you can leverage that or at least do more of the same to make the most of your online marketing and grow your business. Hence, Google Analytics is the key to measuring everything you do in your online marketing journey.

Maybe you've seen or heard about Google Analytics and your eyes glazed over and you didn't think you would ever have any interest in understanding – let alone using – all of the charts and graphs available. If that is the case, so be it... *but* I still want you to get and install the code today. You can ignore it until you're ready to get serious about online marketing. Here's the deal: Install it now, so Google can start collecting all this incredible data. When you're actually ready to look at it a year from now or longer (although your online business might not be around if you wait until "longer" to look at this data), you will actually have data to review. The more data you have, the better and more accurate your ability to see trends, compare previous periods, etc. will be.

When it comes to data analysis, too much is always better than too little.

A Deeper Dive into Google Analytics

If your eyes didn't glaze over reading the last section and you're ready to do more with Google Analytics than simply insert the snippet of code into the header of your website, let's dive deeper into this incredible tool.

Google Analytics will help you clearly understand how traffic is moving *to* your site and *through* you site. It is incredibly powerful, and here's an important word of caution: It will likely deliver more data than you can digest... but don't let that scare you away.

You can select the date range that you want to review, and you should look at full weeks' worth of data. Plus you can set a comparison period (e.g., this month compared to last month). You can see all traffic, direct traffic, mobile traffic, new users, organic traffic (those coming in through search engines), paid ad traffic, etc.

> *The amount of data Google Analytics delivers is both amazing and intimidating. Don't be scared away. At least learn to use the basics to grow your business.*

One of the most important things for small businesses is to check the traffic by location, especially if you happen to have a brick-and-mortar location. For example, you can drill down by country, state, city, etc. Additionally, you'll want to review the acquisition data – how you are acquiring site visitors. In this section, Channels will show you where traffic originated, including the driving keywords. Similarly, Source/Medium will show even more specific information regarding Channels. Finally, you'll also want to keep an eye on Referrals to know which backlinks (links pointing to your website) are driving the most traffic.

Use the Behavior section to evaluate how a particular landing page or blog post might be performing in terms of page views, unique page views, average time per page, entrances, bounce rate, etc. This data really shows how engaged visitors are with your site.

Like I said, Google Analytics is crazy powerful and can also be very, very intimidating, but keep going with it. Perhaps the best way to learn it is to simply log in and spend some time playing around with it!

Facebook Pixel

Full confession: I love you, Facebook Pixel. This is one of my favorite topics because Facebook has changed the entire game of online marketing. In fact, I will even go so far as to proclaim that Facebook Pixel has changed all of marketing!

When you create an advertising account on Facebook, they will assign a piece of code that is custom and just for you. As with Google Analytics, you'll place this code in the header of your website. Now, the Facebook Pixel has a massive amount of power that I will cover in another book, but let me explain one of the Pixel's most useful features right now. This code has the power to remember every single person who has visited your website. When you decide to start running ads on Facebook for a particular offer, you can hop on Facebook and *create an ad to display just to the people who have visited your page!* Why does that matter? It matters because your audience who will see this ad has already been to your site and knows who you are. Remember our earlier discussion about cold, warm, and hot audiences? When you're running ads to a warm audience, your conversion rates for your offer skyrocket!

But wait... there's more. What happens after you've exhausted the audience of folks who've visited your site? Facebook actually has an answer. Facebook knows pretty much everything about every one of its users. It knows how much money we make, our political leanings, how old we are, where we live, who our friends are, what brands we like, what ads we click on, and that list goes on and on and on. Facebook allows you to capitalize on this information in your online marketing efforts. You can pop into

Facebook and request that it takes the list of everyone who has visited your site and create a Lookalike Audience from it. Facebook will then hand deliver to you an audience of people that demographically and psychographically resembles everyone who had previously visited your site. The theory behind this is that the Lookalike Audience will be as interested in and will act on the same things that your actual audience (those who actually visited your site) did in the past. It is effectively creating for you an audience of folks who "in theory" have a predilection to buy from you based on their Facebook profile information.

It goes deeper than just finding lookalikes of people who have visited your site. Think about the endless possibilities of marketing products, webinars, and seminars or whatever your product or service is to people like those who have already *purchased* from you. The key word here is purchased. We all know that people who actually purchase are different from the "Lookyloos" who always seem to just be browsing. Now you have an endless supply of new prospects to market to that look and act really similar to the folks who bought from you in the first place.

Without overstating it, Facebook Pixel practically hands you viable leads on a silver platter.

I don't want to get off on too big a tangent and hijack this book to make it all about Facebook marketing, but I do want to stress that Facebook Pixel and Lookalike Audience building has many applications. Facebook also allows you to upload a list of emails (think client list or email list) and create a Lookalike Audience based on that data. It's incredibly powerful and levels the playing field for small business owners like you with marketing budgets that can't compete with the big dogs.

Website Performance

Before we get into the specifics of "L: Landing" and then move on in The CLICK Technique, I want to make a few more comments about your website (and any page it contains) and its actual performance.

It's important that your site loads quickly. This is another aspect for which Google and your users will give you lots of love. You may think that everyone who comes to your landing page or website is genuinely interested in what you're selling. I'm here to tell you that more often than not, they're only looking around.

So many times I've heard, "I had 25 people come to my site but no one has called or signed up." First, you're going to need a crap ton more traffic coming to your website or landing page than 25 people in order to get enough of an audience to be successful. We frequently get more than a 50 percent opt-in rate (e.g., a visitor signs up to be on an email list, downloads an offer, or takes similar action) on many pages we run at TrafficandLeads.com, but that's after multiple revisions and testing. Remember that thing about data: You need a lot to truly see the trends and make sound decisions.

But I digress: If your page doesn't load quickly, people are not going to wait around for it. They'll move on to the next guy. Additionally, the speed at which your page loads affects your position in search engine rankings. Make sure it's fast. There are ways to test your site's speed, and I've included that in the Resource Section.

Mobile Friendly

Your website must also be mobile friendly – that is, it's pleasing to view on any device from a widescreen monitor to a smartphone. It must be dynamic and reflow properly, depending on the device. According to Hitwise, a reputable company that provides competitive intelligence and consumer insights, in their published report: as of now, approximately 58 percent of overall search query volume in the U.S. is performed on a mobile device. (https://searchengineland.com/report-nearly-60-percent-searches-now-mobile-devices-255025)

Google also gives preferential treatment in search engine results to those who have mobile friendly sites. As you'll recall, Google's main goal is to present its users with the best, most relevant, and professional content possible. I suggest you use

Google's tool to test how mobile friendly your site is (https://search.google.com/test/mobile-friendly). Your site may look just fine on an iPhone but could look really scary on an Android device. Use the tool rather than take any chances.

Creating a Stop 'Em and Grab 'Em Landing Page

Now that we have covered the main items you need to have on any website or landing page you are creating, let's talk specifically about landing pages. Remember what a landing page is and how it differs from your website: It's a very specific page that prompts only a single action from a visitor – click or leave. So, how do you go about creating one that works? There are eight keys to creating a stop 'em and grab 'em landing page, so let's cover each one.

Key 1 – Headline: Do you have an attention-grabbing headline? It's vital that your landing page headline hits people over the head that they're at the right place. Remember: We live in an attention economy now, and people have increasingly limited attention spans. You want your prospect to know immediately that they're going to find what they need. Your headline should address the main issue your prospect has and reassure them they've arrived at a web page that is going to address the issue. In our business coach example, the headline could be: 8 Ways to Cultivate Your Millionaire Mindset.

Key 2 – Description: Give the reader a brief description of your offering. I can't stress "brief" strongly enough. The visitor to your landing page will make a decision to stay or go within a matter of seconds. Even if you present information that is relevant to what your visitor is looking for, if you drone on and on... and on, and don't spice up your content with bullet points and line breaks for easy reading, the user will tire quickly and start their search over. Get to the point and address your visitor's pain with a few points, accentuated with easy to skim bullet points.

Key 3 – Images: If you don't know it, nothing but words scares people! Dress up your page with great images that drive your point home. I have a client who handles fire insurance claims. We put a gigantic image of a burning house in the background, so as soon as the visitor arrives at the page, they know they are at the right place. With that, they can focus more on reading the copy.

Key 4 – Even Better: If an image is good, a video is great. Before you even think about complaining about the effort to create a video, I'll stop you. I know it seems like a daunting task, but it will increase the conversion rates on your landing page. So it's up to you to decide if increasing sales is worth some extra effort to create a video. That said, it should be a *short* video. (Do I have to mention attention economy again?) Additionally, video is an invaluable tool for building that all-important "know, like, and trust" factor that will help your prospects get comfortable enough to take the action you want them to take and to open their wallet and pay you.

Key 5 – Information: You must collect *their* information. Getting the visitor of your landing page to hand over their contact information is the creamy middle of your marketing Oreo. You need to have a form on your landing page asking the user for all the information you need to provide your product or service.

Caution: This is a trust game, so you should only ask the visitor for the information that you need to take the next step. While I'm telling you not to presume they'll know what to do, I'll also tell you that people aren't stupid. They'll know immediately if you are over-reaching in your request for information. When I'm filling out an online form, I'm fine to provide my name and email address – even my phone and address depending on the nature of the request – but it's not my job as the prospective consumer to tell you how I heard about you (at this point) or the last time I put a cute sweater on my cat. If that happens, I'm moving on to the next provider. If your goal is to add them to your mailing list, just get their name and email address.

Key 6 – The Button: Getting visitors to click "the button" is the most important thing you can do on this landing page. Lucky for you, I know how to make that happen, which is why they call me "One-Click Lindsey"! If you can get your visitors to enter a few key pieces of information and click "the button," then you have turned that traffic into a lead. If you follow all the steps, that lead will then be begging to be turned into a paying customer, client, or patient.

So what should that button look like? It should be a very bright color so that it won't be overlooked or missed. It should have a definitive action statement on it like "Schedule Now!" or "I'm Ready to Change" or "Help Me Create a Millionaire Mindset!" Do not use words like "Submit" (often a default) or "Enter" or "Okay." Do any of those words make you want to jump into action and click emphatically? Yeah, I didn't think so.

Key 7 – Testimonials: I want you to be sure to pin your medals to your chest and show them off proudly. Do you have testimonials, security symbols, certifications, or other items that will bolster your credibility? If so, make sure they are displayed on the bottom of your landing page. They show prospects that you're as awesome as you say you are and allow people to feel more comfortable (think: trust factor) sending you their information and making that "One Click."

Testimonials are easy enough for anyone to get, but a lot of entrepreneurs don't ask for them! Maybe they feel uncomfortable asking, but people are usually very happy to say something positive about you and your product or service, provided, of course, you've done a great job. So ask!

Key 8 – Dead End: Yes, you want to have a dead end on your landing page. In other words, you don't want to offer any navigation or links to other sites or pages on your landing page. That may seem counterintuitive; however, trust me on this. View your visitor as a child who can't focus. You want their 100 percent undivided attention on "the button" and giving you that "One Click," nothing else. If they wander away via navigation or other links, chances are you'll never get them back. Their only option on your landing page is to click or leave. That may sound harsh, but if they're not interested in making that "One Click," they probably were not the right prospect to begin with.

Get 'Em Clicking!

- A landing page is not your home page. It is a very specific page designed for a very specific offer, encouraging visitors to take a very specific action.
- Your website and corresponding landing pages must look completely professional. Period.
- Implement both Google Analytics and the Facebook Pixel on your site NOW! They are both free and provide you with

killer data that will enable you to truly be an online success.

- Your website performance – both loading speed and mobile friendliness – will positively or negatively affect not only your users' experience but your search engine ranking as well.
- A killer landing page needs a great headline, brief description, images (or better – video), a way to collect visitor information, "the button," and credential builders.
- Your landing page must also be a dead end with no other links or navigation. Essentially, visitors click or leave.

Chapter 3

Irresistible Offer

At this point, you've generated a ton of curiosity about your products and services through your great content, and you've provided a great place for them to *Land*. Your website has everything it needs to keep your visitors engaged: it's quick, mobile friendly, and professional.

Keep in mind that those who land on your website probably aren't quite ready to do business with you yet because they probably don't know, like, or trust you yet, so you need to build up that comfort level with a little thing called an "irresistible offer." Other names for this all-important part of The CLICK Technique are lead magnet, opt-in offer, freebie, or list builder. Essentially, an irresistible offer is a piece of valuable content that you're willing to give the website visitor in exchange for their contact information (typically just their email address).

While it's irresistible, your offer isn't quite "free." The goal of this offer is to gather contact information, so you can put them into your email marketing funnel. Their email address is the "currency" for your offer. You want to be able to continue to market to them and move them through your sales funnel. Your offer is the foundation for all of your future marketing – your end goal isn't just to get their email address but to warm them up and convert them to become a customer, client, or patient.

Additionally, your offer – it could be a free report, email drip sequence, videos or mp3s, a relevant checklist, an infographic, etc. – continues to convey your professionalism and shows off that you know what you're doing! Your offer must be valuable to your prospect, but it must also build the "know, like, and trust" factor to be successful and for you to ultimately be able to convert those who sign up into paying customers.

> If you don't have an irresistible offer as part of your online marketing, you're wasting your time and money!
>
> If your irresistible offer isn't in a pop-up, you're also wasting money: 80% opt-in via pop-ups!

I recommend having at least one irresistible offer on your website, but a business that is serious about online marketing will have multiple irresistible offers, as many of my clients do. You'll probably have a generic one, but depending on the ads or social media posts that are targeting and driving prospects to you, you may segment the audience by their interests, having different landing pages and different offers.

Take my client, Julie, a naturopath. To start, she has an overall irresistible offer for those who land on her website. Website visitors include folks who want to see what Dr. Julie is about, listen to her podcast, and check out her services and other articles. All of these visitors are greeted with the irresistible offer: "14 Steps to Living a Healthier, Energetic Lifestyle." But for those who have a specific issue with estrogen deficiency (who find her based on those targeted keywords that we'd uncovered in our research, and we know they're getting to her specific page based on our Google Analytics review), they receive the very specific irresistible offer we created, "The Ultimate Estrogen Deficiency Guidebook."

As your business grows and you learn more about your best customers and how they are finding you and visiting your site, it only makes sense that you'll begin to segment these prospects based on their very specific issues and their very specific pain points. Ultimately, to continue growing your business, you'll have multiple irresistible offers!

Additionally, you may need to test your offer. The first one you create may not be as irresistible as you think it is and may not resonate with your page or site visitors. But don't worry. There are rules to follow to really increase the likelihood that your offer truly is irresistible!

Where to Place Your Offer

There are three main mechanisms for presenting your irresistible offer: a dedicated landing page, a content upgrade, and a pop-up.

You would give away your irresistible offer on a landing page if you wanted to drive some traffic to it. For example, let's say you want to build your email list and you have a webinar you want people to opt in for. (Remember: They "pay" for your webinar with their email address, so that's how you'll build your list.) You would create a landing page (using all the tips covered previously) offering people the chance to sign up for the webinar and telling them how great it is and how they are truly going to benefit from it. You would run paid Facebook traffic to this page, knowing the message on your advertisement matches the message on your page, and in theory, the folks who clicked on your ad would sign up for your webinar. You can drive any kind of traffic to a dedicated landing page/irresistible offer combo. The point is that you know what temperature the traffic is and where it's coming from, so you speak to them and their pain points.

Content upgrade is a really cool place to give away an irresistible offer. Let me share how my client, Dr. Julie and I approached this. One of the first things I did when Dr. Julie came to me was to log into her Google Analytics account and found that over 500 people a month were coming to a blog post she had written about estrogen deficiency. (Sidebar note: While Dr. Julie didn't know much about deciphering Google Analytics, she did use the code on her site. She didn't really know how to review the data it gathered, but I did! Let me reiterate how important it is for you to have Google Analytics on your site.) Dr. Julie was shocked to learn that so many people were coming to her site based on this keyword. So what did we do? We put some shine on the blog post so that it was extremely professional and chock full of great information. Next, we created the irresistible offer content upgrade I mentioned called, "The Ultimate Guide to Estrogen Deficiency," and every single person who came to this page was shown the opt-in to this offer. We put an opt-in box with a picture of the report on the left and a place for them to enter their information on the right, and knowing that these people had read the entire article and assumed they wanted more, we would offer them a "content upgrade" – even more content about the topic they were looking for.

The opt-in rates went through the roof! At least 40 percent of the people who were coming from Google were signing up for that email list. By knowing what it was that people were actively searching for, we were able to customize the perfect path to get them to be red-hot leads.

Finally, the least popular but perhaps most effective mechanism is the lightbox pop-up. A lightbox pop-up is a web form advertisement box that appears on top of the webpage that you are viewing. When it appears, the rest of the background and web page is darkened until you enter your information or close it. I know. I know. Everyone hates pop-ups, they feel sleazy and salesy, and "you never fill them out or pay attention to them..." until you do. Until you actually see a pop-up on a website for an offer you can't resist. An offer giving you content that you *must have* and can't get anywhere else. It's at these times you are excited and happy there was a pop-up because you used it to get your hands on that juicy content.

We have seen our clients' conversion rates for their irresistible offers increase by 84 percent just by implementing a pop-up. That means that 84 percent more emails are being gathered simply by implementing this annoying little thing. They work so well because they feature one clear call to action, they catch your visitor's attention, and they have the ability to capture visitors that are on the way out. It's not hard to get a pop-up on your website. If you're using WordPress for your site, I recommend a plug-in called Thrive Themes. If you aren't in WordPress, I've used a piece of software called Optin Monster that works pretty well.

Quick Note: Google has released an update that they may punish you for utilizing a pop-up, especially on a mobile device. However, per their announcement and testing through our client's websites, if pop-ups are used responsibly, it should not hurt your search engine rankings. Therefore, make sure your pop-ups are not spammy or difficult to dismiss and you should be on your way to collecting more email addresses.

Rules for Successful Irresistible Offers

Remember: Most people who visit your website are just looking around. Giving them an offer that is really, really enticing is your only chance of snagging their contact information before they leave your site and never think about you again. Of course, you want them to click!

First, your offer must be consumed by your prospect. If they simply hand over their email address but don't actually review your offer, you're losing them from the start. In that regard, your offer should be reasonably short – long enough to do the job of continuing to build their interest and trust in you but no so long that they don't read or review it. Keep in mind the attention economy we all live in. For example, a 300-page book – while that may seem incredibly valuable on the surface – will probably not be consumed. They'll quickly put it aside to read later... but they never get around to doing so.

Similarly, if you offer a 20-day e-course, it's too long for your prospect to stick with it and consume all of the content. You have to give them a big bang for their buck (i.e., their email address), but it must be easily consumable. In my case, my offer is a five-day course in The CLICK Technique, but it also includes the opportunity to join a private Facebook group, so prospects can also consume at their own pace. Your offer has to be short, sweet, and to the point!

Next, your irresistible offer has to have one big promise on which you deliver. Your goal is to solve one big promise rather than 25 small ones. That's very similar to the consumability rule. In my case, the promise of The CLICK Technique is that it creates a strong online marketing foundation. Or in Dr. Julie's case, it's one big promise of providing what you need to know about estrogen deficiency. Too many promises will confuse and muddy your marketing message.

Additionally, your irresistible offer should be one big promise that you'll solve over time, and it should always speak to the end result that you'll deliver. For example, maybe your offer is a checklist of how to organize your home and reduce clutter. The end result you'll deliver is less stress, feeling lighter, and having more time since you're not coping with daily disorganization.

> *In our attention economy, two important rules for your irresistible offer are: easily and quickly consumed and immediate gratification!*

The third rule for your irresistible offer (and this is true of all of your marketing) is to speak to people's pain points. If you don't know what they are or you don't know how to articulate them, you can start by surveying your list. Ask them! You can also ask them to prioritize a list of the most common pain points your customers, clients, or patients may face. Facebook Ads are another way to survey your prospects and existing customers to determine their pain points and the level of discomfort they cause. I use Amazon book reviews a lot for my own research on various topics. You can peruse the comments left on relevant book titles to see how people are responding and what they're saying about how they may be struggling with the very problem that you solve.

Fourth, your irresistible offer must offer immediate gratification. In addition to living in an attention-driven economy, we all want immediate gratification. For example, the offer "10 Weeks to Your Ideal Weight" won't work very well as an offer, if at all. Sure, it's an admirable goal, but it's too long term for a successful irresistible offer. You may think it's better for them to take their time and get a bigger end result but save that for future marketing. It's a better lead magnet to solve a teeny problem that everyone has because people will be much more likely to opt in on that offer even if a solving a bigger problem would ultimately garner greater benefit. A better example would be "8 Unconventional Secrets to Losing Weight and Keeping It Off." Remember: short attention spans!

Next, your offer must have a high perceived value. This can sometimes be a bit difficult to achieve, especially since we're focusing on solving a small problem. The solution may not seem to have a lot of monetary value. Consider what you would sell this for if you weren't giving it away as your irresistible offer. Also since you're solving a problem or easing a pain point, consider what the prospect *would* pay for this information. Include the cost. Don't lie and inflate the value because people will see right through that, but be certain to include the value on your landing page or pop-up.

Finally, the last rule for a successful irresistible offer is that it always, always, always demonstrates your expertise on the topic and sets you apart from your competition as the best go-to person. Your offer must be *applicable* to your business or your blog. In my case, although I might love gardening, it would make no sense at all for me to tie my offer into my hobby. You're getting their email address and delivering great consumable content that will solve their problem, so you want to position yourself as the expert so that when they're ready to buy, they're going to buy from you. Additionally, through your email sequence, you're going to continue to let them know that you are the best person for the job.

Irresistible Offer Examples

If you're scratching your head wondering what you can use as an irresistible offer, here are some ideas:

Reports and Guides: These are the most common offers I see, and while they can work really well, you also have to be very careful with them. Why? Google. It can work to your benefit but can also work to the benefit of every single person online. Your offer must be unique so that website visitors can't just Google the information you're providing instead of giving you their email address. Our example of "8 Unconventional Secrets to Losing Weight and Keeping It Off" seems to provide a solution to weight loss that you can't just hop out to Google and find. It comes across as a unique answer to a common problem. You really have to have a secret to give away or really good information and pitch it in such a way that downloading your report immediately seems like the only way the website visitor will have access to this information.

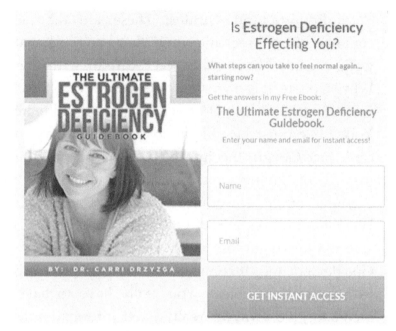

Cheat Sheets or Handouts: I personally like this type of offer a lot because it's often very useful and prospects are quick to click to download. These give you the opportunity to present a lot of valuable information in a very digestible fashion, making them even more attractive because they're easily consumed.

For example, "Ten Steps to Publishing a Highly SEO'd YouTube Video." With this type of offer, you are providing the exact process to solve a prospect's pain point, so they're always more likely to click to download it.

Template or Swipe File: Again, this is attractive to prospects because you're doing the work for them. They don't have to put in a lot of thought or effort, and let's face it: we all love shortcuts! "Hey, give me your email address, and I'll send you 25 Facebook Ads that are highly converting!" Of course, I'd personally bite at that. Perhaps "20 Simple Steps to Producing Your Own Podcast." When you itemize steps or a process, it's not only attractive to a prospect, it is content that is relatively easy to create as well.

Tool Kit or Resource List: Similar to a template, this type of irresistible offer gives your prospect useful information that they don't have to research for themselves. It's another shortcut for them, and in our attention economy, anything that saves time will generate that download click. For example, "10 Ways to Balance Your Hormones to Lose Weight." This isn't something that a prospect can easily find on their own, and when you've already set yourself up as the expert, they'll know it's coming from a good source.

Video Training: People learn differently, but video training tends to be far more attractive than reading for a lot of people, making this type of irresistible offer more... well, irresistible! No matter what you have to teach or share, it is not that difficult to create a professional-looking video in which to do so.

Free Trials: I really like this one for products that fall in the SAS (software as a service) genre. You are actually letting your prospects use your product as means of introducing it. For example, a 14-day free trial works amazing well. Of course, you have to have a really solid product. I recently interviewed the creator of accounting software for small business on the Traffic and Leads Podcast, and his product is so awesome that people convert to buy because they've already spent two weeks getting to know it, testing it with their own invoices, etc. and have already invested some of their own time with it.

Quizzes or Surveys: I find that people like to test their own knowledge and share their opinion, so these also work well as irresistible offers. Two programs you can use for these include Interact (www.tryinteract.com) and Lead Quizzes (www.leadquizzes.com). People really do love to take quizzes, and in order to get the answers, they'll need to provide their email address. You can create a quiz or survey on practically any topic. I recently took a quiz about parenting and also recently created a quiz for one of my clients about "entrepreneurial style." This isn't high school anymore; people actually *love* quizzes.

Give-aways: These are hands-down a great irresistible offer. After all, who wouldn't want the chance to win something really cool, like an iPad? However, these come with a big caveat: You can and likely will get a lot of response and collect a lot of email addresses, but these will also be un-targeted, and as soon as the campaign is over and folks learn they didn't win, they'll unsubscribe from your list *unless* they were truly interested in your product or service in the first place, regardless of your give-away. So with this irresistible offer, first it has to be really valuable, and second, it has to be really relevant to your business. Everyone will bite at an iPad, but not everyone is your target audience.

A great example of a give-away was for a client of mine who runs a natural living online store where she sells all-natural products. Her give-away that drives opt-ins and website visitors is a product from her store. Chances are pretty good that people who don't care about natural deodorant would never opt in to win a container of it. Therefore, this contest is perfect: She is able to hone in on those who are interested in natural products and build her list with those people.

Challenges: These are becoming very popular because, as everyone likes quizzes and surveys, people also tend to have a competitive streak. For example, "Sign up for a 30-day green smoothie challenge and we'll all support each other to drink one green smoothie a day." Work-out a day, write a piece of content a day, etc. Then you follow up with an email every day during the challenge to encourage them to keep going. Dovetailing a private Facebook group with a challenge also works well. You should create very specific rules for it and shut everything down once the challenge is over to prevent "hangers on" who don't continue to engage. A word of caution: This offer will take more of your time as you will need to be continually interacting and cheering on participants.

(See the Resource Section for the link to my podcast about challenges for an interview I did with an entrepreneur who specializes in making challenges rock to grow your business.)

Facebook Group: This is a great way to bring a community together, and you'll get more exposure since Facebook will show your posts more often in streams than it will show your page. Those who join feel like they can speak more freely and be more open since their comments are not shown on their personal profiles. If your irresistible offer is membership in a private Facebook group, you must ensure that it's closed and emphasize that it's private (regardless of your topic or focus or your tactic to allow people to join). Facebook currently allows you to pose questions before allowing people to join. You'll want to make those relatively easy to answer, but at least you'll know that potential members will be engaged enough to answer three questions. If people aren't willing to do this, they probably won't make comments and become a valuable member in your group or as a prospect to grow your business. As with challenges, this is another type of irresistible offer in which you'll need to invest more time with posts or Facebook Live broadcasts for the group. If you'd like to see an example of this in action, make sure you join my private Facebook group at:

www.clicktechniquegroup.com

Waiting List: While not one of my personal favorite irresistible offers, this one makes a lot of sense and can work really well if you are releasing new software or a book, for example. It allows you to build some buzz before the release date. This can also work in tandem with a challenge (e.g., "Get on the waiting list to be part of the next Green Smoothie Challenge!")

Free Quote: This one strikes me as a little boring because anyone can get a free quote, typically just by asking. However, a carpet cleaning client of mine employed this irresistible offer successfully. It happened in two steps. First, prospects filled out information about their house (e.g., number of rooms, type of carpet, presence of pets, stairs, etc.). With that complete, the next page prompted for the name and email to receive the quote. Prospects' expectation may have been that the quote itself would populate on the second page, and at this point, they may have spent a minute or two completing the information, so they were more likely to complete the process to get the quote.

Simply asking for a name and email for follow up contact to provide a quote or consult is definitely *not* an irresistible offer. Ditto to "Sign up for my newsletter." Although that may have been attractive in the very early Stone Age days of the internet and email, that is not irresistible at all!

The Two-Step

Typically the sequence of events for a successful irresistible offer has been: Paid traffic like a Facebook Ad to landing page to email address submission to receipt of offer followed by going into an ongoing email marketing sequence of five to ten email messages in which you'd nurture them and entice them to take another step, all while building that ever-important know, like, and trust factor.

There's a bit of a change in the world of irresistible offers that is working really, really well, and I call it the "two-step." I now have clients sending prospects from a Facebook Ad to a landing page that contains about a 15-minute video. For example, "How to Make More Cold Call Sales Today." The prospect enters their email address and they get the video that does, indeed, follow all of my rules for an irresistible offer: it's consumable (only 15 minutes), makes one big promise (more cold call sales), speaks to the end result (master cold calling), immediate gratification (watch now and employ the tips), it provides tons of value (who doesn't want to improve cold-calling techniques), and it sets the person off as a professional in the way they deliver the video.

Imagine the power of a prospect's click leading right to your calendar to schedule an appointment!

As the prospect is on the edge of their seat, thinking, "This is amazing information," and loving the video, the next message is: "By the way, I will give you an exact script, regardless of the industry you're in, if you sign up for a free consultation today. I'll send it right to you if you get on my calendar by clicking the button below."

Wow. That button click is generating a *direct appointment* on your calendar. Within the moment of delivering the first value, you're offering a second value – the payment of which is your chance to speak with this client directly!

Usually the first step in this process is a video of some sort, but it can also very effectively be done in a webinar as an irresistible offer that delivers a ton of value in a short time and in which you promote "one more thing" at the beginning, in the middle, and at the end, and that one more thing is for them to schedule an appointment with you. In this way, you're getting them to do a lot more than hand over their email address. You can close more sales quicker when you get people on the phone.

Get 'Em Clicking!

- To remain engaged and continue to build a relationship with prospects, you must have an irresistible offer on your website.

- Page visitors don't really know you yet, so they are unlikely to spend money on your product or service. Your irresistible offer works to demonstrate your expertise and the value of your product or service.

- Make sure you deploy your irresistible offer in a pop-up. (No whining!)

- You'll probably have multiple irresistible offers as your refine the targeting and segmenting of your list.

- Your irresistible offer must adhere to these rules: must be consumable, offer one big promise, address pain points, offer immediate gratification, have high perceived value, and demonstrate your expertise.

- There are plenty of types of irresistible offers you can use. Pick the one that may make the most sense for your business and make sure it follows all the rules.

- Consider using the "two-step" technique in which your offer (typically a video) is directly on your landing page and the "click" for more information leads them to your calendar to schedule an appointment with you directly.

Chapter 4

Cultivate: The Power of Email Marketing

At this point in the process, you've generated curiosity, given your prospects a great place to land, and offered something irresistible enough for them to "pay" you with their email address. That may seem like a lot, but it's only the tip of the iceberg in the process. You've taken all of those steps and now have an email list. The list itself was never – and is never – the goal. The goal is to cultivate these prospects to convert them into paying customers, clients, or patients!

Keep in mind that prospects have to know, like, and trust you before they'll open their wallets and hand you cash. They are probably not quite ready to buy at this point, even though you may have a killer irresistible offer. You must continue to build credibility with them in order to successfully close the sale and, more importantly, keep nurturing the relationship so that you'll always be top of mind with them, so they're always turning to you to solve their problems and ease their pain.

The very best way to cultivate a relationship with your prospects is through email marketing. Now don't think "used car salesman forcing pricing on you" when I say email marketing. Email marketing is also *not* sending out bulk emails to as many people as possible, with the vast majority of them snagged in spam filters. Email marketing is a professional conversation with people who have already expressed an interest in talking with you. Since they've handed over their email address, they are allowing you to have that conversation through the privacy of their inboxes. You're communicating, not spamming, through email marketing.

I'll be honest right here and tell you that creating your autoresponder campaign or campaigns takes a bit of work up front, but the best news is that once you create it, it can work for you behind the scenes for years without any effort on your part.

Autoresponder Emails

You'll be sending two types of emails to your list. The first one is an autoresponder email. For example, you have a website visitor who clicks to download your irresistible offer. In your email provider system (e.g., MailChimp or Constant Contact, etc.), you can then set up automated replies that are delivered in a prescribed sequence and at pre-determined times. For example, the first email

> *99% of the people who visit your website will not call you, will not fill out your "contact us" email form, and they sure won't "sign up for your newsletter." You have to offer something to grab their email address. The money is in the list.*

after opt in might be triggered *immediately* as a thank you for downloading the offer and welcome with teaser copy on what they can expect in future emails.

Your product or service will dictate the sequence of messages. Some products and services do not lend themselves to a hard sell or an early sell (i.e., trying to close too soon without having established enough trust or having set yourself apart as the person who can truly solve their problem). In this case, you might send three emails (every day or every other day) with great content that's providing value and cultivating the relationship.

After that, your fourth email will prompt engagement (e.g., "reply with your biggest struggle with weight loss," or "what questions do you have about the training?") from the recipient. When people engage, they are one step closer to trusting you! Your engagement request email is one of the most powerful ones you can send.

I typically advise my clients to repeat this sequence: three emails with amazing, valuable content and a fourth that prompts for engagement. This is a very soft approach, and the goal is to let prospects get to know you better, always building the credibility and trust factors.

(See the Resource Section for a link to sample autoresponder emails that you can use as an idea starter or springboard for your own autoresponder emails.)

Depending on your product or service, you may want to take a harder approach with a more

Your product or service will dictate how long your autoresponder series will be before you try to close the sale.

accelerated sales cycle and "ask for the close" sooner in the sequence. This may be especially useful if your irresistible offer was a free trial. In this case, you might send two emails with valuable content with the third email being a related promotion or to ask for the sale followed by a repeat of that sequence.

Autoresponder Example

Earlier, I introduced you to Dr. Julie and her "Ultimate Guide to Estrogen Deficiency" irresistible offer. Once a prospect clicks to get that guide, they will receive a series of nine emails that continue to provide really valuable content that continues to build Dr. Julie's credibility:

- Email 1: Welcome email making sure they received their download and letting them know she will be checking in on them in the next few days.
- Email 2: A few words on what Dr. Julie specializes in and a video about how important it is to embrace change and make new habits.

- Email 3: A video on how to get tested on a few common ailments that are most common with estrogen deficiency.
- Email 4: A complete guide on what to shop for at the store and a video on how to make smoothies. The email ends with reaching out to them to connect with her on social media and introducing them to her podcast.
- Email 5: A personal email reaching out to the readers asking them to respond to her about what their greatest struggle is when it comes to diet. This is the oh-so-important engagement email.
- Email 6: Starts with a client testimonial about how Dr. Julie's tips have made her feel better than ever before. This email finishes with multiple tips and tricks on sleep and exercise.
- Email 7: An email telling them about her practice and information on how they can be her patient via Skype if they don't live reasonably close to her in Canada. A video on supplementation is included.
- Email 8: An email about exercise with a free guide to a week of exercise.
- Email 9: A final email wishing them well, inviting them again to connect with her on social media and letting them know (and here's the key!) that she will be adding

them to her weekly email newsletter, so they will continue to receive valuable content from her.

As you can see, each email in the sequence provides valuable information. The main goal in the sequence is to give, give, and give some more. The majority of the emails in the sequence give information, with only two of them (#4 and #5) asking the prospect to take action (join on social media and respond describing a challenge).

The key is to build the relationship, and following this method works!

Broadcast Emails

Unlike the autoresponder emails that drip out according to a prescribed schedule and with a pre-determined message, broadcast emails work like newsletters. They are delivered at the same time to your entire list. The most effective broadcast emails are sent at the same time each week and can recap your latest, greatest content. The name of the game with broadcast emails is "continually and forever."

Don't worry about being bogged down every week with your broadcast email. Instead, you can plan one day a month when you'll work on your broadcast emails. You decide what content you will include and create weekly emails for the entire month. You can then pre-schedule them to be sent on a particular day of the week and at a particular time.

This is an ideal approach for consistency, and consistency is critical to the success of your email marketing. If you skip weeks, your prospects and customers are going to notice and start to unsubscribe. I also don't want you to be concerned about the best day of the week on which to schedule your broadcast emails for

> The key to broadcast email success: consistent delivery... forever!

delivery. Some research indicates that most email newsletters are read on Tuesdays, but that actually may not be best for your business. For example, if you operate a brick-and-mortar business as well and are in the business-to-consumer (as opposed to business-to-business) spectrum, emails sent just before the weekend might work best. You can also review the analytics offered by your email system that show when emails are opened to determine the best day and the best time of day (i.e., mornings vs. evenings) to schedule your email. Let me repeat: Consistency is far more important than day or time!

As for content, your broadcast emails don't need to be long... in fact, they shouldn't be. For mine, I typically include a timely message (perhaps holiday related), my one piece of *Curiosity* content for the week, and a link to my site with my tagline. In addition to consistency of delivery, consistency of content makes it more readable (consider how print newspapers are assembled: location of news, sports, comics, etc. are always in the same place), and it also makes it easier and faster for you to create. You'll be following a pre-set outline each time.

Here's the thing: If you're following The CLICK Technique and are dedicated to making one piece of content that sparks curiosity, then you have your content for your broadcast email. It can be exactly the same. Chances are so slim that the video you uploaded on YouTube or your recent blog article was read by most of the people on your list. Quite frankly, even if it was – and they remembered it – they will appreciate you emailing them your latest content, so they don't miss it next time.

Consider these tips for what to include in your broadcast email newsletter:

- Blog post: Highlight your latest blog post or piece of content. Give your audience a sneak peek of the content with a link back to your site to drive traffic.
- Don't be formal: Remember, you're having a conversation, so envision writing your email to one specific person. Your language will be more relaxed, and your readers will feel a connection with you.
- Bulleted Lists: Avoid long paragraphs. Keep it short and simple and easy to scan. Keep in mind that the majority of

recipients are reading on mobile devices.

- Testimonials: This is my favorite thing to include in my email newsletters. It's a great way of showing your expertise in your craft while demonstrating a point.

Email Marketing Head Trash

I mentioned using challenges as an irresistible offer, and I frequently post them with my CLICK Technique Facebook Group. I'm usually pushing folks to email their list at least a minimum of once a week. Again, frequency and consistency are the linchpins of successful email marketing.

However, when entrepreneurs are starting out with email marketing, there is a lot of resistance with the frequency aspect. They are paranoid that they'll be "bothering" people or that people will quickly tire of "being sold to." Well, yes, people *will* quickly tire of being sold to, so your emails should be providing value rather than asking for the sale all the time. When you provide value, ultimately, your product or service pretty much sells itself. If you follow my process for creating and sending your emails (i.e., awesome content!), those on your email list are going to want to hear from you. They will want you to sell to them, so they know how to get more of you!

Regardless, by law (Can-Spam Act), all broadcast emails must contain a way for recipients to unsubscribe. When you work with a service like MailChimp or Constant Contact, the unsubscribe button is built in automatically, so you don't have to worry about breaking the law with your email marketing. Additionally, once someone unsubscribes, those systems will not allow you to inadvertently send them future emails.

Now... about those unsubscribes. Do not obsess about them! Your email service will send you notices about the unsubscribes via email. I suggest you set up a special Hotmail or Gmail email account to which to send those notices and then never check that email. Yes, I mean ignore them completely! You can take a peek at the analytic report offered by your email service perhaps to check the reason why people are unsubscribing, but otherwise, I strongly suggest you don't worry about unsubscribes. In fact, you should be happy every time someone unsubscribes because it means they weren't really a good fit in the first place, and you've freed up space for people with whom you resonate and with whom it makes sense to build relationships!

> *Don't take unsubscribes personally. They simply indicate that you weren't the right fit for that prospect. Plus they leave more room for prospects who make sense for your business!*

Get 'Em Clicking!

- The money is in the list, and using email marketing is the ideal way to cultivate your relationship with prospects.
- Don't think "used car salesman" when you think about email marketing. Instead, simply have a conversation with readers about how you can solve their problem.
- Autoresponder emails are delivered in a prescribed sequence and at pre-determined time intervals.
- Depending on your product or service, you may not ask for the sale or promote an offer in your autoresponder series; however, you should ask for engagement as you're building the know, like, and trust factor.
- Broadcast emails are those that are sent to your entire list (or an entire segment of your list) at the same time. They often work like newsletters.
- Consistency is the key to successful broadcast emails – the same day and time each week with pretty much the same layout.
- Get rid of email marketing head trash. Don't worry about "bothering people" and ignore the unsubscribes!

Cultivate

Chapter 5

Keep Going

Recall, if you will, my daily conversations with my chiropractor neighbor. As I told him then and will now tell you: it takes time. The CLICK Technique will not change your profit margin overnight or in a week. In fact, nothing will. You must *Keep Going*! If you do and are consistently following the steps in the process I've outlined for at least six months, I know your business will change for the better and forever.

Full confession: While I've helped my clients earn millions of dollars, I was guilty of not implementing this technique in my own business. The cobbler's kids have no shoes, right? When I finally decided to put my money where my mouth is and follow my own advice, it truly changed my business… and I know it can change yours as well.

I've done this enough to know that online marketing takes time. When I started, I put my head down and told myself, "You're going to produce amazing content for a year. If in that time, nobody likes a Facebook post or reads a blog or if my email list barely grows, then I'll quit." Of course, as I'd seen multiple times with my clients, it did not take nearly that long to reap the benefits of The CLICK Technique!

Be a Superhero

Yes, it can be nerve-wracking to put yourself out there with videos and personal blog posts and ask people to follow you and like what you have to say. However, I want you to decide to be a superhero. When my son was two, every morning for three months he decided to be a superhero. He refused to wear anything other than the half dozen superhero shirts we'd purchased at Walmart. His grandparents bought him adorable Gymboree shirts, but despite my pleading, those remained in the closet. Superhero shirts only, thank you very much.

As a superhero, he abandoned his own name and adopted the name of the superhero of the day. He'd alter his voice, asking my husband how a particular superhero might sound and then do his best to mimic it. Two-year-old lowering his voice as much as possible to declare, "I'm Batman." Cute. But I digress.

When you're starting a new business or launching a new marketing campaign, it's easy to feel like you're unstoppable. You're excited, motivated, convinced there is no way you can fail. Bound out of bed each morning, excited to take one more step toward your entrepreneurial success and the freedom that brings. However, doubt creeps in and momentum is lost. Sales may stagnate, no one engages with your social media, and your hard work seems to be producing little. There's an easy temptation to give up and abandon your great ideas, right?

Back to my son: After months of proclaiming to be a superhero, he still could not fly; he had yet to thwart a villain; he constantly had to remind everyone to use his superhero name. Piled on  that, his parents actively tried to convince him every day to quit being a superhero. None of those factors and despite a frustrating lack of forward momentum toward his superhero goal, he never quit.

I want you to have that same attitude: ***Wake up every day and decide to be a superhero!***

Running your business and conducting marketing campaigns to generate leads are long, slow endeavors. Persistence is the key to success. Tell yourself every day, "Today, I am going to be a superhero!" Especially on the days when you don't really feel like it. Continue to create content; continue to follow each step of The CLICK Technique. The

Wake up every day and decide to be a superhero in your business and with your email marketing!

strategies work, but you have to stick with it and *keep going*. The entrepreneurs who reflect my son's persistence are the ones who ultimately succeed!

Persistence Pays Off

Consider the story of U.S. Olympic swimmer, Simone Manuel who competed during the 2016 Olympic Games in Rio de Janeiro. Many people may remember her as the first African American woman to win a gold medal in an individual swimming event (100 meter freestyle). Additionally, she won gold anchoring the 4x100 medley relay team. Simone won two silver medals as well, individually in the 50 meter freestyle and as part of the 4x100 freestyle relay team.

According to her mother (as quoted in an article that appeared on the *Absolutely! Fit & Fab* website), Simone got up every day as a youngster and got ready to go to swimming lessons. "She isn't any different in a lot of ways but she is more determined. She makes up her mind. She will do anything to be successful and get it done." Her mother, Sharron Manuel continued, "Simone never complained. She hated to miss swim practice even when she was sore or tired. She never said she didn't want to go to practice. Simone would set a goal and was willing to work hard to reach her goal and have that delayed gratification."

Will you be as dedicated and determined as Simone in the way you run your business and handle your online marketing? Simone sets a great example and one you should emulate. You won't win Olympic medals, but you will succeed in your business, and that's your ultimate goal.

Get Up Every Time, No Matter How Hard You Fall

When you're running your own business, you are going to get knocked down... or you are going to trip and fall at some point. Sometimes, you'll fall hard, and it's going to hurt. Perhaps it is going to happen when you are really striving to attain a huge goal. The key to succeeding is to get back up... no matter what.

Bear with me while I share another inspirational story of Olympic athletes, this time in figure skating. Chinese pairs skaters, Zhang Dan and Zhang Hao competed in the 2006 Winter Olympics in Turin, Italy. They were in second place after the short program, trailing the favored Russian pair. They decided to "go big" in the long program and attempted a quadruple salchow jump throw just over one minute into the program. Zhang Dan fell hard on the landing, smacking her knee, and sliding across the ice, hitting the boards like she'd been checked into them. She got up and tried to continue but seemed unable. Broadcasters commented that there was no way they could continue after such a nasty fall. It was, in fact, painful to watch. They stopped the music. Her partner guided her sobbing across the ice where they were met by the team trainers and coaches.

The trainers determined that if she wanted to, she could continue. She wiped her tears, blew her nose, and they returned to the ice and she did some warm-up skating. The music was re-queued and the pair continued their routine... executing every other move perfectly, including several more difficult jumps and other challenging throws. They ended to a standing ovation, finished second in the long program and won the silver medal.

Despite a painful fall (literally and figuratively) on the world's biggest stage, Zhang Dan got back up, and persevered. It ended with success.

When you get knocked down, no matter how bad it seems, get up, wipe your tears and blow your nose if needed, and concentrate on proceeding and working to execute the next task before you to the best of your ability!

Get 'Em Clicking!

- Marketing – any marketing – takes time to yield results. Do not give up. Keep going for at least six months.
- Wake up every day and decide to be a superhero in your business!
- When you started your business, you had a sense of being unstoppable. Hang on to that.

- Keep in mind the story of Simone Manuel (and so many other Olympic athletes like her) who had the determination to keep training in order to reach the podium.
- When you get knocked down, be like Zhang Dan and get back up and keep going!

Keep Going

Chapter 6

To Hire or Not to Hire

Now that you fully understand The CLICK Technique, I'm sure there is still a burning question in your mind: Does it make sense for you to create and implement your plan (whether you do it or someone on your staff) or should you outsource this aspect of running your business to an outside agency?

My immediate answer to that is that you can succeed either way. Absolutely, and I have no doubt about that! After all, that's why I created The CLICK Technique for small businesses to use and have shared it in this book.

As with every business decision you make (in fact as with every decision you make in life), there are pros and cons. In this case, there are pros and cons to hiring someone to handle this for you in-house or outsourcing it. Notice I said hiring someone to handle this for you in-house. You're an entrepreneur, so I know you are extremely busy. The first decision you have to make is whether or not you are going to leave marketing on your personal plate as a day-to-day responsibility for *you*. That may not be the best use of your time, but that really depends on your own expertise and is a decision that you'll have to make.

So, the decision is whether to hire an employee or outsource your marketing to an agency. Full transparency: As the founder of an online marketing agency, it's hard for me not to lean hard in that direction, but I will be objective in reviewing the pros and cons so that you can make the best decision for your business.

Agency Benefits

Despite what you may be thinking, one of the biggest benefits to hiring an agency is the cost. Am I suggesting that hiring an agency will be lower cost? Yes. That is exactly what I'm saying. To start, an agency will bring with it a team of people to serve you, and those team members have their particular areas of expertise. In the case of my own company, it starts with me as an online marketing expert and strategist along with another person with the same expertise and skill set that I have.

Using an agency for your online marketing has lower cost than hiring an in-house employee.

We both have a broad knowledge in many, many areas, including SEO, pay-per-click (PPC), marketing funnels, landing pages, copy, and email marketing. Plus, we also have an in-depth technical background, so we can get right into the guts of a site and do what needs to be done. Add to that, hosting and domain name expertise. Personally, I've been doing this for over a dozen years, so I've been with it pretty much from the ground up.

Now, I also have a copywriter on my team. Yes, I could write the copy for a 12-step autoresponder sequence, but I'll be the first to admit that I cannot do it as efficiently as my copywriter can.

I also have someone who specializes in SEO, and he lives that day in and day out. He's aware of everything that's going on in the world of SEO, and more importantly, he stays abreast of all the changes and is aware of all the updates Google makes. Additionally, I have a PPC specialist who knows everything there is to know about pay-per-click.

Next, my company also has graphic designers, so clients bring me their branding ideas, and the graphic designers really bring them to life. This can be a real area of struggle for those entrepreneurs who handle this in-house and for other agencies that happen to outsource this aspect of online marketing.

Add to the mix a Facebook marketing expert. I personally love Facebook Ads, so I do a lot of work in that realm, but my employee is a real whiz at this and is always educating herself on the latest, greatest updates and best practices when it comes to Facebook advertising.

This team is always staying up-to-date, and as I mentioned and you probably already know, the world of online marketing is a constantly moving target. In fact, I recently had a meeting with my PPC expert and she mentioned a new approach that even I had yet to hear about. The simple truth is it is impossible to have one person on your own team – even if that person would happen to be me – who can know everything there is to know and do everything there is to do to create a truly viable marketing funnel and make your online marketing work for you.

> *An agency will deliver a team of experts who can stay up-to-date in their specific areas in the ever-changing world of online marketing.*

So let's say you find a great person who really knows as much as they need to about all of these different aspects. You'll first be paying them handsomely for their expertise because if they know everything they need to know and can get their hands dirty with implementation and execution, they will be worth quite a lot. Your expense to bring this in-house of course doesn't end with salary. Consider your recruitment costs, hiring costs, training costs, and oh yeah, benefits like paid holidays, vacation, and sick time. Plus you'll need someone to manage this person, and if that will be you, you must consider the value of your time in doing so.

Also keep in mind the cost of a mis-hire. Maybe the person doesn't turn out to be the expert you thought they were, so you have to start the process all over. All that money you spent recruiting, hiring, and training the wrong person just went down the drain.

There is no doubt that having employees is expensive! Yes, I love my employees, but when the holiday season rolls around, those paid days off take a financial toll, and that adds some emotional stress as well. As an entrepreneur, you have to admit that when there's time off, there's a lot of money going out in the form of paid time off with no productivity happening and limited, if any, revenue coming in as a result.

Another benefit to hiring an agency is that you get the diversification that comes with having a team of experts at your disposal. Again, finding someone who has the diversified skills that I mentioned when I described my own team would be really, really hard to find; really, really expensive; and really, really hard to keep... unless what you pay them and the benefits you offer are through the roof. Can you afford that?

In-house Benefits

Now that I've promoted using an agency, I'll get off that soapbox and discuss why you might want to hire someone in-house rather than outsourcing your online marketing. Yes, there are benefits to this approach.

First, there will be product, service, and company expertise. When we bring on a new client, it does take time for me and my team to really get to know them and understand their product or service and their market. It can take time to be able to create effective marketing funnels, gather feedback, and develop new ideas. And we have to get feedback from the staff and perhaps the owner(s), so there is some time investment needed to discuss marketing strategies and results with the agency.

An in-house employee, being fully immersed in your company and culture, will know it better than an outsider.

An employee may be able to do all of this more quickly and with greater immersion. Certainly an agency can do it; however, it will take time, and time is money. Additionally, it will never be as immersed to the degree that an in-house employee can deliver.

Additionally, access and knowledge about the company's culture is very useful when it comes to online marketing because of being "on location," so to speak. An in-house employee can be shooting photographs and posting immediately that will boost social media. These photos help your Facebook pages and other social media platforms truly reflect the personality of your company and be less business-like. They go a long way to building the know, like, and trust factor.

Again, as an agency, we do this, but the client has to provide the photos. We tell them what we think they should be shooting and rely on them to provide decent pictures. There is a time lapse between our request and the posting. Facebook and Instagram are really personal, so pictures are a must, but the photography is not something we can provide for them. An in-house person is physically there, and they'll know what's "moving and shaking" and what's prime for social media.

Finally, there is a feeling of being in control when you hire an in-house person for your online marketing. I know when some clients hire my agency, they feel like they've tossed the ball into our court and all they can do is hope we generate traffic and leads for them. Obviously, with an employee, you can see them all day, every day and have an immediate sense of what they are doing. They are completely integrated on your team, so you feel like you have control over this critical part of your business.

I certainly understand that last benefit, yet having covered the benefits of both approaches, of course, I'm still going to suggest you hire an agency. I truly believe that our clients view us as part of their team, but it does take some time to get to that point in the relationship.

What to Ask!

While I'm espousing hiring an agency to handle your online marketing, you want to avoid hiring the wrong one. In the same way that hiring the wrong employee can be costly and result in a lot of wasted time and money, hiring the wrong agency can leave you with the same problem.

Perhaps you are already using an agency to help you generate traffic and leads, and you're facing the scenario I just painted: You feel like you've thrown the ball into their court, and you aren't getting any feedback; you aren't sure what they're working on; you sense they get annoyed with your calls and emails; and you feel like they expect you to simply sit on your hands and wait for them to get back to you. If that's the case, it may be time to find a new agency.

Whether you're hiring an agency for the first time or you want to replace your current agency, here are the questions you must ask.

What is your process? What should I expect the first month? What should I expect the second month? When can I realistically expect traffic and leads to start flowing? What will it all look like?

Be sure to set expectations, so you know what the agency will and will not deliver.

When you sign up at TrafficAndLeads.com, we create a spreadsheet that we share with you online, we itemize the months and what strategies and tactics we're going to employ each month, and we're constantly updating this and emailing information to clients. We also use an internal project tracking software, so all team members can effectively communicate and collaborate. Additionally, when we're running Facebook or other paid ads, our clients get updates at least three times a week. This can get expensive, and we know that clients want to know what's happening and what the results are.

Who is on your team? Who will be working on my account?

In the case of TrafficAndLeads.com, I do most of the selling, but then I do hand clients off to an account manager after we go through an onboarding process. This is a benefit because, although you won't be speaking directly with the PPC or SEO expert, you will have a single point of contact who is going to bring that all together for you. This is a far more efficient model than trying to work with ten different people in the agency. You may also want to meet the account manager to ensure that you will be compatible working together.

What is your client communication process? I've just outlined what we do, but this is something about which you want to be really clear, so set the expectation about communication up front. Will they use shared spreadsheets or share access with their project management systems (like Basecamp or something similar)? Or do they use emails or weekly or monthly phone meetings? I'm not suggesting that one method is better than another; however, you definitely want to ask this so that you know what to expect from the outset.

What analytics do you track? You really don't want to work with an agency that is only tracking what I call "vanity metrics" like traffic. Of course, you want to track traffic, but you also must track (or your agency must track and report to you) things like conversions, engagements, click-through rates. These are the metrics that actually demonstrate whether or not there is improvement. Again, online marketing is

Be certain there are metrics in place, so you can effectively and accurately measure progress and improvement.

a long game, and it's like planting seeds and waiting for them to grow and produce. You'll only get the results in the latter months, but you want to see constant improvement. Back to the seed analogy, you want to be certain you see it sprout and then grow a bit each week in order to know you'll get to harvest later. Ask the agency which metrics they think you should be watching, especially to ensure that they are doing their job.

How do you track SEO effectiveness?

TrafficAndLeads.com maintains a spreadsheet of all of the keywords we are pursuing for each client and the associated URLs. Twice each month, we provide reports on keywords that specifically show where they were the previous months and where they are now, so they can see and track the improvement. Of course, in the interim, we're discussing this during other conversations we have with them, and they get the report like clockwork on the first and 15th of each month.

What's included in your fee and what creates an additional charge?

You also want to ask any online marketing company about the expectation of expenditures for advertising, aka the "ad spend." Plus you'll want to verify if this is included in the fee or if this will be an additional charge. I've had clients complain to me that they were told by another agency the fee would be $1,000 per month only to be hit with an additional $1,000 for the ad spend. There is nothing wrong with charging the ad spend

Know what is included in the fee from the outset to avoid unpleasant surprises as you go through the process.

separately and outside of the agency's fee; however, you want to be certain to ask, so the expectation is clear. You will also want to be clear about what the maximum ad spend is that you are willing to pay each month.

Can you show me successful examples of your work?

Finally, you definitely want to ask about this. Ask for examples of ads, emails, funnels, etc. You should also ask for referrals – names of clients they've worked with in the past and follow up with these people to ask about their experience and satisfaction. You can also look at their websites and social media platforms to be certain they look professional and to ascertain what sort of engagement they've been generating.

In addition to asking for referrals, you can also look for reviews of the agency you're considering. For example, you can Google, "TrafficandLeads.com reviews" to see what other clients have said about the service. Make sure you put the power of the internet to work for you here because you might find some interesting information posted. You can and should use this same tactic before hiring any company to do work for you either professionally (for your business) or personally. Referrals are great, but you can pretty much be certain that you are going to get referrals from people who really liked the company you are considering. A little due diligence on your part will go a long way.

Growth Takes Time

So, what can you really expect from an online marketing agency? This is a tricky question for any agency to answer because it depends on the ad spend and your goals. Perhaps a better approach is to set your budget and then find out what the agency can do for you within that amount.

For example, if someone comes to TrafficAndLeads.com with a $2,000/month budget and tells us they want us to do everything, including content marketing, social media marketing, some pay-per-click, Facebook Ads, plus the ad spend, things are going to move slowly. That said, we can do it. We'll outline a plan based on your budget (although in the example, for that budget, we'll be crossing a few items off the list). Based on your budget, we may ask that you handle some of the aspects of the plan, but there will be an implementable plan.

Keep in mind my earlier garden analogy when it comes to your online marketing. You'll be planting some seeds to start, and it is going to take some time before you see flowers blooming. The seeds need time to grow, mature, and bear fruit. The same is true of online marketing. It will take a few months before you see results and then reap what you've sown. This is true of any online marketing agency you may hire. Be patient with them and trust the process. If they guarantee overnight or quick results, be cautious. Be very cautious. It may be what you want to hear, but that claim has no foundation in the reality of how online marketing works.

> *Be patient and trust the process. Online marketing is a long game. Results take time.*

Trust the process and let the agency do its work. Just because your PPC campaign isn't resulting in a lot of leads during the first two weeks, in the case of TrafficAndLeads.com, we're actually in there daily making modifications and perfecting the campaign. Maybe your first irresistible offer doesn't work; we'll have to go back and try something else. There is a lot of trial and testing in any type of marketing to see what works, and online marketing is no exception.

As long as your online marketing agency is communicating with you, even to report that an approach didn't pan out as hoped or expected, have patience. Like I said, online marketing is a big test to see what is going to resonate and generate results. Honestly, if I knew what would work for every company in every industry right off the bat, I'd be far wealthier and would have already retired! The truth is, the same thing does not work for every single company or in every single industry.

The need to test, tweak, retest is true for every agency. Your demographic is just that – yours. So it takes time to determine what is going to work well and be most effective for your particular target audience. Did I mention that it takes time?

If you've asked the questions I've listed and you are satisfied with the answers you received, it's time to leave it to the agency, have patience, sit back, and know that you're in good hands and the results – the traffic and leads – will come!

Get 'Em Clicking!

- There are definitely pros and cons to hiring an employee to handle your online marketing in-house or outsourcing it to an agency.

- An agency with a team of experts that covers every aspect of online marketing will be less expensive for the expertise that you'll receive.
- A team of experts, all focusing on their areas of specialty, can stay more up-to-date on the changes and updates that occur than can a single individual.
- On the other hand, an in-house employee will know your product, service, and business more thoroughly and will be immersed in it.
- An in-house employee has the ability to immediately capture (e.g., via photographs) your company culture to post to social media to boost the know, like, and trust factor.
- An agency can become an integrated member of your team, but that takes more time.
- When you decide to hire an agency (or change agencies if your current one isn't working out), there are questions you must ask in order to avoid hiring the wrong agency.
- Be certain you have open channels of communication with your agency and set the communication expectations from the outset.

- Once you've hired the right agency, trust the process and remember that online marketing is a long game and results will not be immediate.

Chapter 7

Online Marketing Head Trash

You have no shortage of thoughts swirling through your head all day, every day. What you focus on and what gets the bulk of your conscious attention drives your outcome. Knowing that, you want to focus on the positive to generate positive results. This is true whether you're thinking about your business, your relationships, or any other endeavors that you may undertake. How you think is how you do.

That's easy to say; however, I also understand human nature. Entrepreneurs are human and are subject to doubts about running their businesses. Those doubts are what constitute head trash, and I want you to get rid of it! If you don't think you have head trash, you're lying to yourself... and anyone else who may listen. We all have head trash.

I definitely struggle with it, so that's why I'm including a chapter about it. I have felt everything I'm about to cover, and I'm nearly 100 percent positive that you have, too. This is especially true when it comes to online marketing. Online marketing, as I've said, is a long game, and waiting for results can be difficult. It's that time of waiting when head trash can really take over.

For business success, you have to create a group of people following and surrounding you –

your tribe – and that takes some time. You will never do this overnight or even in a day. When you use content marketing, especially when you don't put a lot of ad spend behind it, to create your tribe of people who are going to give you business, it's simply going to take time. While you're waiting to harvest your traffic and leads, there is quite a lot of head trash that is going to pop into your mind.

> Head trash contains the doubts and negative thoughts that swirl in your brain. Every entrepreneur has head trash.

Comparisons

First, you'll probably start comparing yourself to others. This tendency is nothing new. It starts in childhood. She has prettier hair than me. He's a faster runner than me. And it keeps going through adulthood. They have a nicer house than me. They probably make more money than me. The truth is none of that may be true, and it's merely your own imagination about it. You don't actually know the other side of the story. She may have prettier hair, but you're smarter. He may be a better runner, but you're a better chess player. You get the picture.

It's also a really bad idea to compare your online marketing strategies and tactics to your competitor or to any other business. What works for them might not work for you. Recall please, how I already covered how much testing is needed in all marketing to determine what is really going to work and resonate with *your* target audience. Moreover, it's also a bad idea to assume that anyone else's online marketing approach is really working for them. You may not really know how much profit their online marketing is generating. They may be failing miserably and you don't know that.

The best thing you can do is turn it off and stop comparing yourself to others. Create your plan and implement it. Then stick with it and don't worry about what Joe happens to be doing on his site. Just stick to your plan. This is also where the "shiny object syndrome" comes into play – where you're quick to be distracted by the newest thing that comes along, causing you to take your eye off your own plan and upstage what you're already doing. Turn off this noise!

Fear of Rejection

It does take a lot of guts to put yourself "out there" in your online marketing, especially with content marketing. There's a lot of fear on the part of almost every entrepreneur that prospects are going to laugh at you or make fun of you.

This is especially underscored in the ability for a prospect to comment negatively on a blog or social media post. I won't kid you, it could happen. But to that I'll quickly say, "So what?" Those sorts of posts are typically made by people with too much time on their hands who are insecure about themselves and try to build themselves up by making negative comments about other people.

Not everyone is going to agree with your opinion or approach, and remember that those who disagree aren't your target audience in the first place. Snarky comments always reflect on the person making them, not on you.

The Right Time

This is a big part of head trash among many entrepreneurs – they are always waiting for "the right time" to post or launch.

I recently sat down with my sales manager and we reviewed all of the leads that were in our various sales funnels. This was a list of entrepreneurs who had expressed an interest in hiring us and working with us. In some cases, we'd provided a quote and never heard back. Honestly, many of these leads had gotten cold – ice cold. When we started reviewing the comments about them in our system, most of those comments were along the lines of "not ready yet" or "call back in six months" or any other delaying tactic that all spelled out one clear message: They were waiting for "the right time."

- I'm going to do it next summer.
- Next winter I'm going to do this.
- I'm going to do it after the holidays.

- I'm not feeling inspired, so I'm going to wait until I do.
- It's just not the right time.

I see so many business owners waiting for the right time. Guess what? There is no "right time" and there never will be. This is true for your online marketing and every other aspect of your business. When you tell yourself that you are waiting for the right time to launch or post or whatever it is you need to do, you are making an excuse that amounts to nothing more than head trash.

Just do it! Right now *is* the right time. Right now is especially the right time to get started with online marketing.

Listening to Everyone Else

This is another big part of entrepreneurial head trash – listening to everyone but yourself. No one knows your business as well as you do, so why aren't you listening to yourself first?

I had a client who really struggled with this. We had a discussion about her website. It was all outlined, looked very professional, and had a great call to action and every component that goes into a really great website. She had approved it at every stage, and we went

Be careful who you listen to. If they're not an expert or not invested in your business, what they have to say doesn't matter.

ahead and built the site. During our discussion, she mentioned that she'd spoken to someone else who didn't like this, that, and the other thing about the site. So instead of listening to my whole team of professionals who'd put their expertise together to build a truly killer website, the client is listening to one other person... who is not the expert.

Once you hire experts, listen to them. If you're not hiring experts, listen to your heart. Like I said, no one knows your business as well as you do. Continuing to solicit outside opinions and listening to others is another form of procrastination.

Talent over Persistence

You assume that talent over persistence is the secret to success.

Let's say you're running an e-commerce site, and you see all these other e-commerce stores popping up, and you feel like they're more successful than you (there's that comparison problem again), but you actually don't know or have any facts or data to support what you're feeling. Even if others are posting comments or sharing photos purporting their success, please remember that anybody can say anything and it might be fake and is probably an exaggeration anyway.

I'm here to tell you that they are not necessarily more talented than you. My clients are successful because they are persistent, and yes, they may certainly be talented but they understand that it is persistence that truly pays off. They stick with it through the cycles of getting a lot of leads, getting no leads, Facebook Ad worked, Facebook Ad didn't work. Regardless of the mistakes or missteps, they know that online marketing works. They keep doing it. They are persistent!

Anyone who has achieved online notoriety and fame started exactly where you are. Their success came because they kept pushing through, kept posting, kept blogging, kept adding to their YouTube channels, etc. They stuck with it, and that's how they got to where they are today. I have no doubt about this. There is no one who hops online and succeeds the next day. There are no "overnight sensations" on the internet. In reality, there is no such thing as an overnight sensation. There is always a lot of work and persistence that went on behind the scenes or unnoticed until the big success happened.

The Spotlight Effect

Putting yourself "out there" can be nerve-wracking. I know; I've been there, too. I know the feeling of starting a Facebook Live broadcast and looking at the "0 viewers" staring back at me. Worse than that: Seeing it tick up to "1 viewer" after a minute only to have it drop to zero again 15 seconds later. It takes a lot of practice to keep smiling at the camera and not fumble over what you want to say or stutter while your brain is screaming, "I'm doing this for zero people and the one person who happened to wander in was so bored, they bailed after 15 seconds!" You're convinced that person thought you were an idiot, and no one else is watching because they already *know* you're an idiot.

If you've felt this way about some of your online posts, blogs, videos, etc. (even if it wasn't live on Facebook), this is the Spotlight Effect and it's a form of head trash. The Spotlight Effect occurs when you think people are observing you and judging you far more than they actually are. It happens because we're limited by our own point of view, so we can only see things through that lens. We put ourselves out there; we struggle to imagine how we look in other people's eyes. We can attempt to put ourselves in the shoes of the audience, but it's almost impossible to escape the feelings of nervousness and the fear of screwing up.

> The reality is that people aren't paying as close attention to you as you think they are. They're busy worrying about who's paying attention to them.

I remember ninth-grade speech class, waiting for my turn to stand up and deliver the speech I'd worked really hard on for a week. As my turn approached, my internal panic was reaching fever pitch. "How is everyone else doing this so calmly," I thought. Then I realized maybe they weren't. Some kids were fumbling their lines, or losing their place, but I wasn't registering that as failure. However, inside their own heads, they were probably screaming, "Oh man. Everybody knows I screwed up."

If I didn't care that somebody else messed up, why was it that everybody cared if I messed up? Bingo... nobody does. It's the Spotlight Effect at work.

Great news: If you hate being a tiny bit vulnerable and putting yourself into a blog post or video, **nobody cares as much as you do.** That's actually a double-edged sword because when you finally pen that perfect blog post or deliver the perfectly scripted and narrated video... nobody cares as much as you do. Become aware of this and understand that people don't care – or even notice – what you are doing to the degree that you think they do.

Everything you do to market your business, even if it's "seen" by hundreds of people will likely only resonate with a handful of them. And when that happens, there will be a real connection between that handful of people and you, not because they're mocking you or focusing on what you did right, but because they're focusing on how you can help them. That handful is your target audience and will very likely become your new customers.

The Pratfall Effect

Perhaps you're worried about making a mistake. In reality, your error can have an endearing quality, and as a result, the audience will like you more!

This has actually been tested by psychologists in a study in which a large number of people were watching a quiz show with various hosts. As part of the test, one of the hosts spilled his coffee. This was the only difference in the various test presentations. At the conclusion, those watching were asked to rate the hosts and which one they liked best. The overwhelming winner was the host who had spilled his coffee. The reason? He came off as a lot more relatable.

You can make this work for you in your online marketing, especially when recording videos and podcasts. (This really won't work for blogs, since errors in blogs simply come off as sloppy.) If you stumble over your line or your cat happens to walk in front of the camera while you're recording, just move on. It makes you more human and more likeable. Don't edit those sorts of things out in the post-production process. This is another reason why Facebook Live and Instagram Stories are so popular right now. There is no opportunity to correct bloopers before anyone sees them. The audience isn't watching something that's highly edited.

However, there are considerations in which this can backfire rather than work to your advantage. You can't be stumbling over your lines to the extent that the audience starts to take pity on you. You certainly can't be stumbling when talking about your actual product or service!

Secondly, in order for the Pratfall Effect to work in your favor, you must be viewed as an expert – someone who knows more than the audience. If whoever is watching you does not view you as a little bit "above" them in your area of expertise, it's not going to be effective. They'll view you as a "regular Joe" or even as someone who knows less than they do.

Taking Out the Trash

So how do you get rid of this head trash?

This is a marathon, so you need to find whatever positivity gas works for you and continually fill your internal engine with it. Personally, I start every day listening to an uplifting podcast to really help set my mind straight for the day.

Consider some of these mantras:

- My success is inevitable.
- I accept challenges with enthusiasm and confidence.
- I always push through failure and find a way to succeed.

Pick your favorite or develop some of your own. Repeat them daily. Post them on your bathroom mirror or computer monitor.

Sign up to receive an inspirational quote of the day in your inbox. Find a day-at-a-time calendar that includes an inspirational message.

Be selective in your reading and make certain what you are reading and putting into your brain has a positive impact on you and your business.

You must surround yourself with positivity. What you focus on is what happens. When you fill your brain with positivity, there is no room (or certainly less room) for doubt and head trash!

Get 'Em Clicking!

- Every entrepreneur has head trash – those doubts that creep in and take over.
- Stop comparing yourself to others. They may not know any more than you do. Don't assume what they're doing is working.
- Get over your fear of rejection. For the most part, no one is going to make fun of you, and so what if they do?
- Stop waiting for the "right time." There is no "right time" and there never will be. Just do it.

- Don't listen to anyone who is not invested in your business or who is not an expert.
- Don't assume talent over persistence is the key to success. Persistence pays off every time.
- Beware of the Spotlight Effect. People aren't paying as much attention as you think they are.
- Use the Pratfall Effect to your advantage.
- Surround yourself with positivity and focus on it. What you focus on is what comes to fruition. Focus on the positive rather than the head trash.

Bonus Chapter:

Facebook for $5.00 a Day

There are a ton of Facebook marketing strategies, but to start I'm simply going to share what you can easily do – and do today – to utilize Facebook marketing without needing to hire a Facebook Ad consultant such as myself. I don't want you to get bogged down with more complex strategies because I know that's the quickest way to stop your momentum, and I want you to *Keep Going*! As with any marketing, it may take three to six months to really see results, but this is a great way to siphon leads off Facebook.

First, ensure that you are using your fan page, not your personal Facebook page. Your personal page may currently have greater reach, so you may be inclined to use that, but be warned: Facebook has policies against advertising on your personal page and if you're caught doing so, your page will be suspended. Use your fan page! 'Nuff said.

On your Facebook fan page, you'll set up a "likes" campaign to increase likes for as little as $1.00 to $5.00 a day. (Hop over to theclicktechnique.com and included there is a mini video training on how exactly to do this.) Keep in mind that all marketing is in place to bring people into your sales funnel, and liking your page on Facebook is step one in getting prospects into that funnel and a little closer to you. Step two is to feed awesome content every day – content they can use and on which they can comment. It's "Marketing 101" – the more people see and get to know you, the more they trust you; the more they trust you, the more likely they are to purchase from you.

When you generate extra special content, you'll want to "boost" it to your Facebook Fans to increase the likelihood that greater numbers of people will see it. You've probably seen the "boost" button on your page. Some marketers will slap your hand if you reach for it, but I say do it. This is a simple strategy that you can do by yourself… and it works!

Give awesome content, beautiful pictures, really valuable information. Don't bore your followers, but encourage them to interact. When it's time to promote an offer, they will be far more likely to opt in because they know you give tons of great, usable information. Ultimately, you want to get them off Facebook and onto your mailing list, so you can effectively market to them.

> *You can launch a Facebook likes campaign for a few dollars a day. There's no reason not to do it.*

To start your Facebook likes campaign, you'll first have to know your avatar – the representation of your perfect client. Before you begin creating a

Facebook likes campaign, you have to be very clear about all of the specifics that make up your avatar. The more specific you can be about the demographics (e.g., gender, location, age, income, hobbies, etc.) the more successful your ads will be... and as you'll see in a moment, Facebook can support all of those specifics and more.

Audience Insights is another really useful Facebook tool. Once you're on the dashboard for Audiences, you'll find another search box that will allow you to once again drill down into very specific information and analytics. Make notes about what you find because you'll use this to create your Facebook likes ad to really appeal to your avatar or ideal customer.

In creating your ad, Facebook will even prompt you regarding your ad's goal (e.g., create brand awareness or local awareness) and considerations (traffic, engagement, video views, lead generation, app installs, etc.). For your likes campaign, you'll select "engagement" and then "page likes." Next you'll select the page for which you want to get likes (your Facebook fan page). Then we'll delve into the audience demographics that you previously uncovered – age, income, what they like, job titles, gender, etc. You can also add a geographic location if you'd like. Facebook really walks you through the process to drill down to exactly what you want! Additionally, since this is a likes campaign, you'll want to be sure to *exclude* people who already like it, so you don't waste your money.

In creating your ad, you can either upload your own images (photos, logos, etc.) or select up to six from the Facebook library. I recommend using three as Facebook will then report on how well they each performed and the cost/like. You'll be able to add a headline and a bit of text. It's short and sweet, so you really want the image to stand out and tell them why they should like your page.

Get 'Em Clicking

- Create and use your fan page, not your personal page on Facebook.
- All marketing is designed to get people into your sales funnel, and liking your Facebook page brings prospects to the edge of your funnel.
- Posting awesome content keeps them moving through your funnel.
- Boost your really special content by spending a few dollars a day.
- Know your avatar before launching a Facebook campaign.

Resources:

Below is a list of links and useful sites that I've referenced throughout the book that you will find useful and easy to refer back to as you are employing The CLICK Technique:

The CLICK Technique Worksheet
https://www.dropbox.com/s/hhvnhvhakltes0d/the-click-technique-worksheet.xlsx?dl=0

Google Keyword Planner
https://adwords.google.com/ko/KeywordPlanner

Google Insights
https://www.google.com/trends/

Yoast SEO
https://yoast.com/

Page Load Testing
Want to know you your website stacks up against the rest? Visit https://tools.pingdom.com for a free website speed test. You can also Google "PageSpeed Insights" for a speed test directly from Google.

Google Mobile-Friendly Testing
https://search.google.com/test/mobile-friendly

Finding content topic ideas:

Peruse these question/answer sites to learn more about what people are asking about in regard to your product or service:

Quora: https://www.quora.com/

Reddit: https://www.reddit.com/

Creating Quizzes:

Use either to build and create quizzes or surveys to use as your irresistible offer.

Interact (www.tryinteract.com) and

Lead Quizzes (www.leadquizzes.com)

Power of Facebook Challenges podcast

http://trafficandleadspodcast.com/power-of-facebook-challenges/

Email Managers

MailChimp: https://mailchimp.com

Constant Contact: www.constantcontact.com

Autoresponder email examples

https://www.dropbox.com/sh/ait09t8trhot5aw/AACvRfraR5WGZvckb6zq0LqTa?dl=0

Creating Pop-ups for your opt-in offer:

Thrive Themes for WordPress:

https://thrivethemes.com/

Optin Monster:

https://optinmonster.com/

Resources

About the Author

Even as a young girl, I loved bringing a business to life and watching it grow. Other girls wanted to babysit, while I worked out the percentage I could charge for getting them jobs and managing them. For me, a lemonade stand was not a "fun" way to waste a summer afternoon; it was a very serious business involving customer acquisition and profit margins. I was born an entrepreneur, and I believe you are either born that way or you're not. I see an opportunity, and I have no other choice but to create the business and capitalize on that opportunity. My husband, on the other hand, just wants a job (so I made one for him).

After years of struggling through being an "employee," I started Web Impakt, which over the last 12 years, I perfected (if I do say so myself). I've led my team to launch everything from simple web pages to enterprise-level systems. I've managed dozens of developers and designers yet, still, have had to roll up my sleeves on a Saturday evening (after all, if you want a job done right, eh?). And most importantly, I've gotten very good at generating traffic and leads, not only for my business but for my client's businesses as well.

Traffic and leads... attracting and cultivating that resource is what it's all about. If you're not doing that, then the engine of your online marketing strategy has no fuel with which to work. But if you're smart and place your focus on driving website visitors to make that ONE CLICK and enter your world, you have a lead. Leads become clients. So, how do you get that one click, and what do you do with it? That's the easiest part: You come to me, and they don't call me "One-Click Lindsey" for nothing! My hand-picked team at TrafficAndLeads.com and I ensure that our clients get the traffic and leads their business needs using proven techniques.

Traffic and Leads specializes in landing pages, email sequences, search engine ranking, newsletters, analytics, social media, pay-per-click ads, websites, blogging ... the list goes on. We know how to utilize the myriad of online marketing options to generate more traffic and leads which produces more paying clients.

I am living a life beyond the wildest expectations of that little girl creating flyers advertising her, "Babysitter's Club." Best of all, I get to spend my days doing the only thing I've ever wanted to do, helping small businesses grow.

Made in the
USA
Columbia, SC